LOS A

Welcome to Los Angeles!

This opening fold-out contains four pages of valuable information, handy tips and useful addresses, and a general map of Los Angeles to help you visualise the eight districts discussed in this guide. On the map, indicated by a star, the ten sights not to be missed if your visit is a short one.

Discover Los Angeles through eight districts and eight maps

A Downtown
B Griffith Park / Los Feliz / Silver Lake
C Hollywood
D West Hollywood
E Beverly Hills / Culver City
F La Brea / Hancock Park / Koreatown
G Santa Monica / Venice
H Pasadena

For each district there is a double page of addresses (restaurants – listed in ascending order of price – cafés, bars and shops), followed by a fold-out map for the relevant area with the essential places to see (indicated on the map by a star ★). These places are by no means all that Los Angeles has to offer, but to us they are unmissable. The grid-referencing system (**A** B2) makes it easy for you to pinpoint addresses quickly on the map.

Transportation and hotels in Los Angeles

The last fold-out consists of a transportation map and four pages of practical information that include a selection of hotels.

Thematic index

Lists all the street names, sites and monuments mentioned in this guide.

ARCHITECTURE

Mission Revival (1890–1915)
Spanish Colonial Revival (1915–30)
Stucco, arched windows and entryways, and red-tile roofing seen in large-scale public buildings and houses. (Union Station, **A** D4; Roosevelt Hotel, **C** B2).
Craftsman/California Bungalow (1900–30)
As seen in Gamble House (Charles & Henry Greene, **H** A2), west Adams, southwest of downtown, and Bungalow Heaven in Pasadena (**H**).
Beaux Arts (1900–30)
Pasadena's City Beautiful movement of the 1920s (Civic Center district, **H** B-C2) as well as downtown from 1900–17 (Biltmore Hotel, **A** B4).
Art Deco (1920s)
Streamline Moderne (1930s)
Very urban and stylized (Wilshire Corridor, **E** A1-4).
International Style (1920s–30s)
Rooted in Bauhaus with horizontal planes of glass, steel and concrete. R. M. Schindler and Richard Neutra (Neutra colony, **B** F3).
Case Study House program (1945–60)
Richard Neutra, Pierre Koenig, Charles and Ray Eames created prefab designs: 21 of the 36 'studies' are built in the L.A. area.
Deconstructivism (late 1970s–present)
Fragmentation and distortion: Frank Gehry's Disney Hall (**A** C4), Thom Mayne's Sci-Arc (**A** D5).

DOWNTOWN LOS ANGELES SKYLINE

March; Kodak Theatre (**C** B2)
Hollywood's highest honors – and biggest party night.
Los Angeles Marathon
→ *Third Sun*
April
Coachella Valley Music and Arts Festival
→ *Last weekend; Indio, near Palm Springs*
Music celebration in the desert with world-class performers such as Prince, Paul McCartney, The Cure...
May
Cinco de Mayo
→ *May 5; throughout the city*
Popular drinking night; historic Olvera Street hosts a three-day celebration the weekend prior.
June
L.A. Pride
→ *Fri-Sun, early to mid-June; West Hollywood*
Parade and live music.
Los Angeles Film Fest
→ *Ten days, mid-June; Westwood Village*
Over 200 feature films, narrative, short and documentary screenings.
July-August
Sunset Junction Street Fair
→ *Second-to-last or last weekend of Aug; Silver Lake* (**B** D4)
Neighborhood party with a stellar music lineup; sunscreen is a must.
Nisei Week
→ *Nine days, over two weekends, mid-Aug; Little Tokyo* (**A** C4)
Sumo and taiko drum performances, gyoza-eating contest, etc celebrate Japanese-American culture.
September
L.A. County Fair
→ *Wed-Sun, through Sep; Pomona, east of L.A.*
Largest county fair in the country; concerts, contests, and tons of fried foods.
October
→ *Oct 31, some events take place the prior weekend*
West Hollywood Carnival in the streets of BoysTown (**D** D3) is the most flamboyant.
November
Dia de los Muertos (Day of the Dead)
→ *Nov 1-2; various locations*
Programs at Olvera Street and Hollywood Forever Cemetery are notable.
Los Angeles Auto Show
→ *Ten days, late Nov or early Dec; L.A. Convention Center* (**A** A6)
Ten-day extravaganza with exhibitions of concept cars.
November-January
Downtown on Ice
→ *Mid-Nov to mid-Jan; Pershing Square* (**A** B4)
Outdoor skating rink.

OPENING HOURS

Government and post offices
→ *Mon-Fri 9am–5pm*
Banks
→ *Generally Mon-Fri 9am–6pm; Sat 9am–4pm*
Stores
→ *Generally Mon-Sat 10am–6/7pm; shorter hours on Sun*

CITY PROFILE

■ Often just called L.A. or the City of Angels, it is the second largest city in the US with 4 million inh. over 467 sq. miles of land ■ Los Angeles is also the name of the Californian county: 4,081 sq. miles; 75 miles of sandy coastline; 10.3 million inh.; 88 cities, which include Pasadena and Burbank
■ Temperate climate year-round: low humidity and little rain; average high 74°F, average low 56°F ■ Time zone: Pacific Standard Time (PST), 8 hours behind London (GMT)

DOWNTOWN SEEN FROM ECHO PARK

SANTA MONICA BEACH HOUSES

GUIDED TOURS

LA Conservancy
→ *523 W 6th St, Ste 826 Tel. (213) 623-2489; www.laconservancy.org; $10*
Walking tours, mostly downtown. Self-guided tours can be printed from their website.
Esotouric
→ *Tel. (323) 223-2767; www.esotouric.com; $58*
Off-beat bus tours themed around famous crimes and cult writers
Starline Tours
→ *Tel. (800) 959-3131; www.starlinetours.com; $*
Double-decker bus tours. The Movie Stars Homes one is the most popular.

WWW.

→ *discoverlosangeles.com*
Official visitors' guide of the City of Los Angeles.
→ *experiencela.com*
Official cultural listings and events calendar.
→ *theguide.latimes.com*
Listings section of the *Los Angeles Times*.

TOURIST INFO

Convention & Visitors Bureau
Los Angeles
→ *685 S Figueroa St* (**A** B4) *Tel. (213) 689-8822 Mon-Fri 9am–5pm*
→ *Inside the Hollywood & Highland complex, 6801 Hollywood Blvd* (**C** B2); *Tel. (323) 467-6412; Daily 10am–10pm (7pm Sun)*
→ *Convention Center (kiosk), 1201 S Figueroa St* (**A** A5) *www.lacvb.com*
Pasadena
→ *300 E Green St Tel. (800) 307-7977; www.visitpasadena.com*
Santa Monica
→ *1920 Main St, Ste B Tel. (800) 544-5319 Daily 9am–6pm* (**G** B4)
→ *Palisades Park (kiosk), 1400 Ocean Ave* (**G** A3) *and Third St Promenade* (**G** A3); *www.santamonica.com*

TELEPHONE

Eight area codes cover L.A. County. Within this guide are used 213 (downtown); 310 (Westside: Santa Monica and Beverly Hills); 323 (Hollywood, Silver Lake); and 626 (Pasadena).
UK to Los Angeles
→ *00 + 1 (USA) + area code + seven-digit number*
Within the US
→ *Dial 1 + area code + seven-digit number*
Los Angeles to the UK
→ *011 + 44 (UK) + number minus the initial 0*

Useful numbers
Police / emergency medical service
→ *Tel. 911*
Directory inquiries
→ *Tel. 411*
International operator
→ *Tel. 0*
Toll-free numbers
→ *Numbers beginning with 800, 866, 877 and 888*

DIARY OF EVENTS

Public holidays
Jan 1 (New Year's Day); third Mon in Jan (Martin Luther King Jr's Birthday); third Mon in Feb (Presidents' Day); last Mon in May (Memorial Day); July 4 (Independence Day); first Mon in Sep (Labor Day); last Friday in Oct (Nevada Day); Nov 11 (Veterans Day); fourth Thu in Nov (Thanksgiving); Dec 25 (Christmas Day)
January
Tournament of Roses Parade
→ *Jan 1; Colorado Blvd, Pasadena*
New Year Celebration.
Rose Bowl Game
→ *Usually Jan 1; Rose Bo Pasadena*
The oldest college foot bowl game.
Golden Globe Awards
→ *Second or third Sun; Beverly Hilton Hotel* (**E** A
Launch of the awards season.
Los Angeles Art Show
→ *Late Jan; L.A. Conventi Center* (**A** A5)
A five-day exhibition ar sale featuring 130+ galleries, museums an arts foundations.
January-February
Chinese New Year
→ *Dates vary according t lunar calendar; Chinatow*
Two-day festival, Golde Dragon Parade, Lanterr Festival (Chinese Ameri Museum), and more.
February-March
Academy Awards
→ *Last Sun of Feb or first*

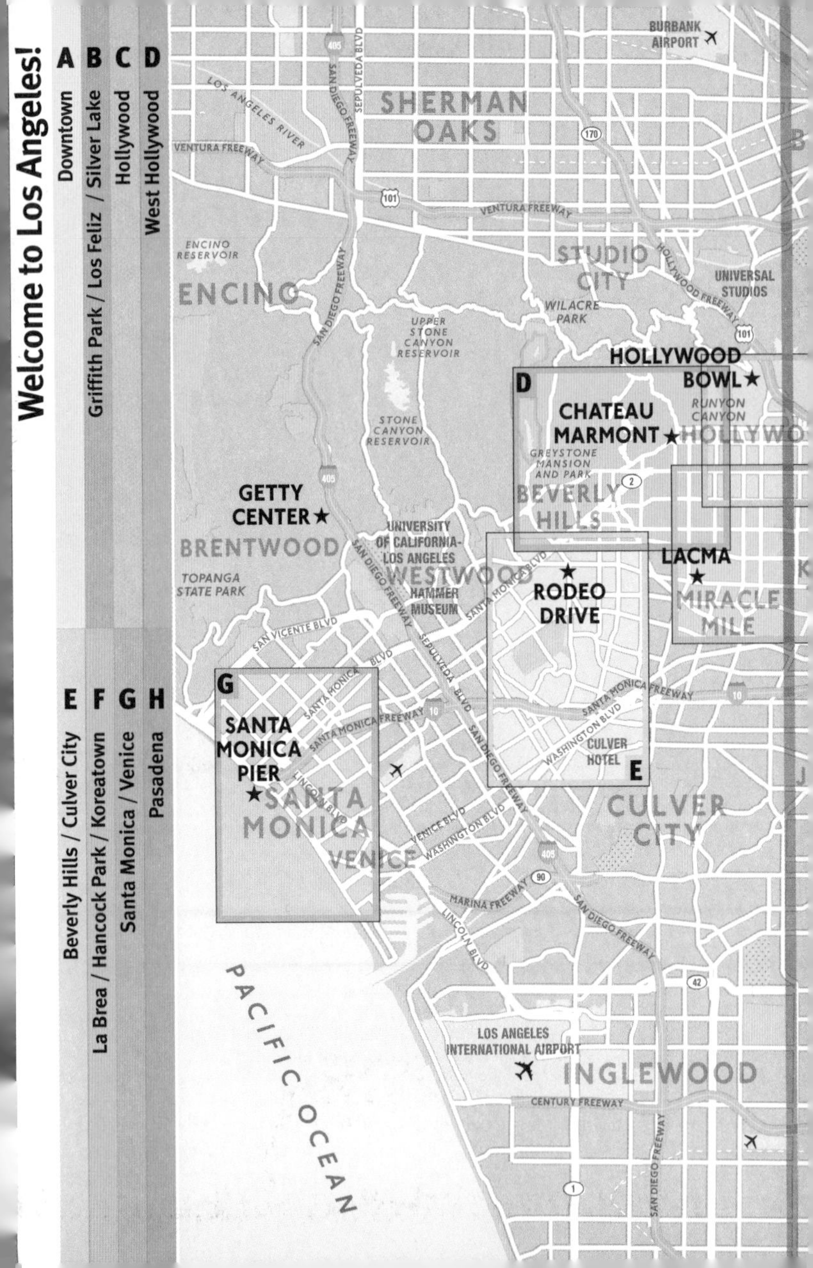

Welcome to Los Angeles!
A Downtown
B Griffith Park / Los Feliz / Silver Lake
C Hollywood
D West Hollywood
E Beverly Hills / Culver City
F La Brea / Hancock Park / Koreatown
G Santa Monica / Venice
H Pasadena
BURBANK AIRPORT
SHERMAN OAKS
LOS ANGELES RIVER
VENTURA FREEWAY
SAN DIEGO FREEWAY
SEPULVEDA BLVD
405
170
101
ENCINO RESERVOIR
ENCINO
STUDIO CITY
UNIVERSAL STUDIOS
HOLLYWOOD FREEWAY
WILACRE PARK
UPPER STONE CANYON RESERVOIR
STONE CANYON RESERVOIR
HOLLYWOOD BOWL
RUNYON CANYON
CHATEAU MARMONT
HOLLYWO
GREYSTONE MANSION AND PARK
BEVERLY HILLS
2
GETTY CENTER
BRENTWOOD
UNIVERSITY OF CALIFORNIA-LOS ANGELES
WESTWOOD
HAMMER MUSEUM
TOPANGA STATE PARK
SANTA MONICA BLVD
RODEO DRIVE
LACMA
MIRACLE MILE
SAN VICENTE BLVD
SANTA MONICA BLVD
SANTA MONICA FREEWAY
10
SANTA MONICA PIER
SANTA MONICA
LINCOLN BLVD
WASHINGTON BLVD
CULVER HOTEL
CULVER CITY
VENICE BLVD
VENICE
90
MARINA FREEWAY
PACIFIC OCEAN
42
LOS ANGELES INTERNATIONAL AIRPORT
INGLEWOOD
CENTURY FREEWAY
1

BRAND PARK
EATON CANYON PARK
BURBANK
GLENDALE FREEWAY
FOOTHILL FREEWAY
ROSE BOWL
PASADENA
H
VENTURA FREEWAY
GRIFFITH PARK
GLENDALE
VENTURA FREEWAY
FOOTHILL FREEWAY
GRIFFITH PARK OBSERVATORY
B
C
LOS FELIZ
GOLDEN STATE FREEWAY
SILVERLAKE RESERVOIR
HUNTINGTON LIBRARY
MOUNT WASHINGTON
PASADENA FREEWAY
HUNTINGTON DRIVE
ALHAMBRA
HOLLYWOOD FREEWAY
ELYSIAN PARK
A
WALT DISNEY CONCERT HALL
EL PUEBLO DE LOS ANGELES
BUNKER HILL
SAN BERNARDINO FREEWAY
MONTEREY PARK
KOREA-TOWN
F
DOWNTOWN LOS ANGELES
SANTA MONICA FREEWAY
SANTA MONICA FREEWAY
GARVEY RESERVOIR
POMONA FREEWAY
EAST LOS ANGELES
JEFFERSON PARK
LOS ANGELES RIVER
SANTA ANA FREEWAY
ROSEMEAD BLVD
RIO HONDO
HARBOR FREEWAY
FLORENCE
LONG BEACH FREEWAY
SOUTH GATE
ROSEMEAD BLVD
SAN GABRIEL RIVER
SAN GABRIEL FREEWAY
CENTURY FREEWAY
CENTURY FREEWAY
LYNWOOD
0
2,5
5 km
1/ 220 000 - 1 cm = 2,2 km

rose Avenue. But L.A.'s e interesting fashion ts are in areas such as one between La ega and La Brea, rose and 3rd, with iculously curated tiques selling emerging, nt-garde designers.

HTLIFE

n neighborhood bears a nct nightlife character: e and hipster in Silver ; gay in West ywood; industry-heavy ollywood. Comedy s and music venues the Sunset Strip; usive velvet ropes k off Hollywood; ntown fills with Lakers and symphony ndees. Bars and clubs ramping up Thursdays he weekend. Evening walks have become easingly popular in ery-heavy districts.

Cultural listings
LA Weekly
➔ *On Thu, free; in news boxes, book- and coffeeshops*
Its restaurants critic, Jonathan Gold, is considered a foodie guru.
Angeleno Magazine / 944 Mag / Los Angeles
➔ *Sold at newsstands;*
Three glossy monthlies covering the city's high culture.

Discounted tickets
L.A. Stage Alliance
➔ *Half-price tickets on its website: www.lastagetix.com*
Center Theatre Group
➔ *Tel. (213) 628-2772; $20 Hot Tix for its performances; www.centertheatregroup.org*

NO SMOKING

Smoking is banned in bars and restaurants, and restricted from beaches, parks and golf courses. Soon outdoor smoking in patios or on sidewalks within ten feet of any place serving food or beverage will be prohibited too.

BEST VIEWS

City Hall
From the 27th floor (see **A**).

Griffith Observatory
Stunning at night (see **B**).

Getty Center
Drive or walk the Getty View Trail, a challenging one-mile hike starting off Sepulveda Boulevard, north of Getty Center Drive (*www.lamountains.com*), (see **G**).

Mulholland Drive
There are ten scenic overlooks along the corridor between the 405 and 101 freeways. Exercise caution at night; there's a reason why the road famously inspires noir literature and cinema.

The Grove (F)
360 panorama from the top floor of the parking lot.

EXCURSIONS

Malibu
➔ *33 miles west of downtown; www.ci.malibu.ca.us*
27 miles of scenic beauty with world-famous surfing (Surfrider Beach) and hiking (Point Dume, Point Mugu, Malibu Creek State Park).

Disneyland Resort
➔ *Anaheim; 27 miles southeast of downtown; http://disneyland.disney.go.com*
Aside from the original park it now has three hotels, Disney's California Adventure Park and Downtown Disney, a retail-dining district. Many forums provide tips on how to maximize the hefty $72 ticket price.

Palm Springs
➔ *109 miles east of downtown; www.palm-springs.org*
This weekend playground and retirement community for movie stars and mobsters has 125 golf courses, spa resorts, hiking, camping. Rates go down in the summer, but many businesses may also be closed.

Catalina Island
➔ *High-powered ferries (1-hr journey) from Long Beach or San Pedro (25 miles from downtown); www.catalinachamber.com*
For snorkeling, scuba diving, kayaking and glass boat tours. Hiking, camping and mountain biking require permits – ask the Catalina Island Conservancy, *www.catalina conservancy.org*. Don't miss the Art Deco event hall known as the Casino and the Wrigley Memorial and Botanical Garden.

HOLLYWOOD

The entertainment industry is a fact of life in L.A. In any part of the city, at any time day or night, one may encounter a location shoot in progress. Be aware that during awards season streets can be closed off for days.

Studio tours

Of the Big Six motion picture powerhouses – Paramount, Warner Bros, Sony, Universal, 20th Century Fox and Disney – only four offer guided tours ranging from the historic (**Paramount Pictures, C**) to one powered by animatronics (**Universal Studios, C**). Note that tours are affected by filming schedules: a visit one day might result in finding a celebrity at work while another might mean multiple closed sets.

Sony Pictures

➔ *10202 W Washington Blvd; Tel. (310) 244-6926; Mon-Fri 9.30am, 10.30am, 1.30pm, 2.30pm; $28*

Two-hour walking tour through the former, much-downsized home of MGM studios. *Wizard of Oz* and *Spider-Man* were filmed here.

Warner Bros

➔ *3400 W Riverside Dr., Burbank; Tel. (818) 972-8687; Mon-Fri 8.20am-4pm; $45*

Widely considered the best studio experience, the VIP tour (2¼ hrs, 12 guests max.) includes a tram ride through back-lot sets where *Casablanca* and *Blade Runner* were shot.

MALIBU

Restaurants

➔ *11/11.30am–2.30pm, 5/5.30–10/11pm. Closing times vary, but Sun or Mon is a typical closing day*

Bars, nightclubs

➔ *Daily 4pm–2am; no alcohol can be sold later than 2am. Bars with larger food menus sometimes open throughout the day*

Museums

➔ *Usually 11am–6pm; late night one midweek night; closing day varies*

MONEY

Credit cards

Widely accepted but farmers markets and some ethnic or long-standing restaurants are cash only.

Budget

Accommodation

Minimum $80 per night at a standard hotel.

Eating out

Ranges widely, from $5 at a taqueria to $300 a head for the 29-course omakase at Urasawa (**E** B1).

Going out

Some bars and clubs apply cover charge, especially if live music is scheduled ($5–25).

Tax

9.75 percent sales tax; 14 percent occupancy tax for hotel rooms (15 percent in Pasadena and Beverly Hills).

Tipping

15–20 percent; usually 18 percent of the bill's subtotal in restaurants; 10–15 percent for taxis; $1–2 per drink at bars.

EATING OUT

Options are as diverse and sprawling as the city itself. Ethnic enclaves such as Little Armenia (**C**), Thai Town (**C**) and Koreatown (**F**) are sought-after destinations, as are the restaurant rows along La Cienega and Beverly.

Specialties

Angelenos have two enduring passions:

Tacos: The traditional Mexican composition of tortilla (usually corn) folded about a choice of meats (grilled steak marinated in salt, chicken, spit-grilled pork, even marinated offal) is served everywhere, from taquerias to trendy bars and roving taco trucks; 'Taco Tuesday' is a popular weekly special throughout the city.

Burgers: It seems every L.A. entity is looking to perfect the American classic, from high-end brasseries to the fast-food drive-thru. Prices range from less than $3 to $20.

SHOPPING

Luxury labels on Rodeo Drive and Sunset Plaza or consignment and vintage stores in Los Feliz and

LITTLE TOKYO / JANM

BRADBURY BUILDING

★ **Elysian Park** (**A** C-D1)
→ *835 Academy Rd*
On the nearly 600 acres of this verdant oasis 2 miles north of Civic Center the Avenue of the Palms and an arboretum are among the many highlights. Nature trails offer appealing views of the city and nearby Dodger Stadium.

★ **El Pueblo de Los Angeles** (**A** C-D3-4)
→ *Bordered by E Cesar E Chavez / N Alameda / N Main*
El Pueblo de Los Angeles commemorates the site of the city's founding in 1781. The 44-acre park includes the preservation of Avila Adobe, the oldest existing home, and Olvera Street, which re-creates a lively Mexican village marketplace. Opposite is the Mission-style façade of Union Station (1939), which continues to function as a hub for Amtrak as well as the city's rail and bus systems.

★ **City Hall** (**A** C4)
→ *200 N Spring St (1st)*
Tel. (213) 485-2121
Mon-Fri 8am–5pm
Standing at 454 feet, this distinguished 1928 terra-cotta-and-granite structure was an exception to an old, seismically vigilant height restriction. The 27th-floor observation deck offers one of the most breathtaking views of the city. Don't miss the beautifully decorated archways and columns of the third-story rotunda.

★ **Little Tokyo** (**A** C4)
→ *Bordered by E 1st / S Alameda / E 3rd / S Los Angeles*
JANM: 369 E 1st St; Wed-Sun 11am–5pm (noon–6pm Thu)
These four square blocks still remain a vibrant center of Japanese culture. Beyond the sushi bars and anime shops, the area is home to the critically acclaimed Asian-American theater group, East West Players, and the Japanese American National Museum (JANM).

★ **Bradbury Building** (**A** C4)
→ *304 S Broadway (3rd)*
Visitors allowed up to the f landing only
The city's oldest comme building, designed by George Wyman in 1893, a towering five-story atriu It is a marvel of glazed b marble stairways, open c elevators and ornate ironwork, all bathed in natural light filtering thro the glass dome above; a favorite film site, it was featured in the sci-fi clas *Blade Runner*.

★ **Los Angeles Centra Library** (**A** B4)
→ *630 W 5th St (Grand)*

↑Map B
A
B
1
2
3
4
SILVER LAKE BLVD
COMFORT INN
W SUNSET BLVD
BERKELEY AVE
SCOTT AVE
MONTANA ST
RESERVOIR ST
GLENDALE BLVD
ECHO PARK
LEMOYNE ST
ECHO PARK AVE
MORTON AVE
SCOTT AVE
MONTANA ST
N RAMPART BLVD
MARATHON ST
N ALVARADO ST
ANGELUS TEMPLE
ECHO PARK
BELLEVUE AVE
HOLLYWOOD FREEWAY
101
W KENSINGTON RD
E KENSINGTON RD
W EDGEWARE RD
DOUGLAS ST
E EDGEWARE RD
N PARK VIEW ST
W TEMPLE ST
W COURT ST
N WESTLAKE AVE
N BONNIE BRAE ST
N BURLINGTON AVE
N UNION AVE
BEVERLY BLVD
S ALVARADO ST
W 2ND ST
W 3RD ST
S WESTLAKE AVE
S BONNIE BRAE ST
S BURLINGTON AVE
S UNION AVE
WESTLAKE
COLUMBIA AVE
WITMER ST
LUCAS AVE
MIRAMAR ST
N BOYLSTON ST
N BEAUDRY AVE
HARBOR FR
W 6TH ST
W 4TH ST
W 5TH ST
S BOYLSTON ST
S BEAUDRY
WILSHIRE BLVD
WITMER STREET
GOOD SAMARITAN HOSPITAL
W 7TH ST
BUNKER HILL
S FIGUEROA
S FLOWER ST
WESTIN BONAVENTURE HOTEL
BUNKER HILL STEPS
CALIFORNIA
110
ELYSIAN PARK
EL PUEBLO DE LOS ANGELES
CITY HALL

A

Downtown

In a city famously without a center, Downtown has played its part as the hub of L.A.'s civic and financial enterprises. Bound loosely by three freeways and a river, the area also encompasses several historically ethnic enclaves, a mere sample of the city's diversity. Redevelopment has taken effect over the last decade: MOCA and Gehry's Disney Hall have transformed the cultural skyline just as unprecedented numbers moved into converted lofts and luxury residences. An enlivened nightlife includes some of the most buzzed-about restaurants, bars and club venues.

Prices given throughout this guide are average prices for a main course only.

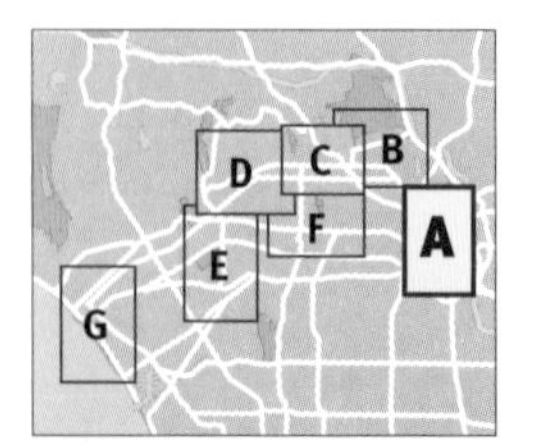

PHILIPPE

CHURCH AND STATE

RESTAURANTS

Philippe The Original (**A** D3)
→ *1001 N Alameda St (Ord)*
Tel. (213) 628-3781
Daily 6–10pm
This 1908 shop offers the French dip sandwich: beef, lamb, pork, ham or turkey varieties are ordered single-dip, double-dip or wet. $6.

The Original Pantry Cafe (**A** B5)
→ *877 S Figueroa St (9th)*
Tel. (213) 972-9279
Daily, 24 hours
Angelenos come to this 1924 institution for their round-the-clock fix of hearty American fare like roast beef dinners, rotisserie chicken, hotcakes and eggs. $8.

Daikokuya (**A** C4)
→ *327 E 1st St (San Pedro)*
Tel. (213) 626-1680
Mon-Sat 11am–midnight (1am Fri-Sat); Sun noon–'until soup is gone'
This tiny, first-come-first-served noodle house serves rice dishes, sushi rolls and gyoza, but ramen fanatics come for the bowl of egg noodles and Kurobuta pork in a rich porcine broth. $9.

R23 (**A** D4)
→ *923 E 2nd St (Vignes)*
Tel. (213) 687-7178
Mon-Fri 11.30am–2pm, 5.30–10pm; Sat 5.30–10pm
In a loftlike space in the Arts District, with contemporary art on the walls, you can sit in Frank Gehry chairs and have fantastically fresh sushi or sashimi, fried sawa crab or ribeye steak with ponzu. Reservations advised. $12–20; sushi $4–12.

Pacific Dining Car (**A** A4)
→ *1310 W 6th St (Witmer)*
Tel. (213) 483-6000
Daily, 24 hours
This 1921 railroad car evokes its era with mahogany accents and brass fixtures. The hamburgers are great but don't miss the chocolate soufflé. Another branch is in Santa Monica. $13–20.

Church & State (**A** D6)
→ *1850 Industrial St (Mateo)*
Tel. (213) 405-1434; Tue-Fri 11.30am–2.30pm, 6–10pm (11pm Fri); Sat 6–11pm
This former Nabisco Biscuit Company space with exposed brick and industrial ducts is a stylish brasserie, where chef Walter Manzke cooks such classics as pig's ears, snails, house-made rillettes and terrines. $20.

Patina (**A** C4)
→ *141 S Grand Ave (1st)*
Tel. (213) 972-3331

TINA

L.A. LIVE

FUGETSU-DO

Tue-Sat 5–9.30pm; Sun 4–9.30pm (on performance evenings: Tue-Sat 5–11pm; Sun 4–10.30pm)
Chef Joachim Splichal's flagship restaurant, inside Disney Hall, is a walnut, glass and curved bentwood setting where you can enjoy sautéed foie gras, lobster, roasted Colorado lamb and other seasonal fare. $35.

PUBS, MUSIC VENUES, GALLERIES

Seven Grand (**A** B5)
→ *515 W 7th St (Olive) Tel. (213) 614-0737; Mon-Wed 5pm–2am; Thu-Fri 4pm–2am; Sat-Sun 7pm–2am*
This Irish-style dark wood pub with taxidermied jackalopes specializes in premium whiskeys (there are 271 to choose from), small-batch bourbons and cigars. Live bands and a 150-year-old pool table add to the diversions.

The Mayan (**A** B5)
→ *1038 S Hill St (Olympic) Tel. (213) 746-4674; Fri-Sat 9.30pm–2am; call for special events; www.clubmayan.com*
Built in 1927 in the style of a pre-Columbian temple, this architectural gem doubles as a concert hall and a sizzling nightclub with three levels of dance floors. Serious salsa dancers and live orchestras converge on Tropical Saturdays.

L.A. Live (**A** A5)
→ *800 W Olympic Blvd (Figueroa); Tel. (213)763-LIVE*
The entertainment campus has hotels, restaurants, clubs and theaters. Staples Center is home to five professional sports teams including the Lakers; the Grammy Museum chronicles the recording history; Nokia Theatre features top music acts and hosts the Emmy Awards, and there is the sports-themed restaurant ESPN Zone.

Gallery Row (**A** C4-B5)
→ *Spring and Main (between 2nd and 9th)*
With only three galleries at the time of its designation in 2003, this district now boasts nearly 50 spaces dedicated to contemporary and local art; Downtown Art Walk is held every second Thursday of the month from noon to 9pm.

SHOPPING

Grand Central Market (**A** C4)
→ *317 S Broadway (3rd) Tel. (213) 624-2378 Daily 9am–6pm*
This historic 1917 open-air market reflects the culinary diversity of the city; the stalls now also include a multicultural array of prepared foods like kebabs, burritos and pupusas.

Fugetsu-Do (**A** C4)
→ *315 E 1st St (San Pedro) Tel. (213) 625-8595; Daily 8am–6pm (7pm Fri-Sat)*
For three generations this family-owned sweets shop has made the area's best wagashi (rice flour-based confections).

FIDM Scholarship Store (**A** B5)
→ *919 S Grand Ave (9th) Tel. (213) 624-1200; Mon-Fri 9am–6pm; Sat 10am–4pm*
Bargain shopping along Santee Alley can be rewarding but in the tamer environs of the Fashion Institute this store has brand-name apparel, fabric and accessories – all donated by nearby designers and merchandisers.

Kinokuniya Bookstore (**A** C4)
→ *123 Astronaut E. Onizuka St (1st); Tel. (213) 687-4480 Daily 10am–8pm*
The L.A. branch of the global chain stocks the full inventory of anime and manga. Twee stationary and art supplies are plentiful.

American Apparel Factory Store (**A** C6)
→ *747 Warehouse St (7th) Tel. (213) 488-0226 (ext. 1459); Mon-Fri 9am–8pm; Sat 10am–7pm; Sun noon–6pm*
This corporate headquarters has an on-site store where factory overruns, samples and irregulars are sold at discount. Also occasional flea market clearinghouse events.

Indie style in Chinatown (**A** D3)
Young bohemia has set up of apparel, jewelry and home accessories boutiques. Notable shops are: **Welcome Hunters** (*451 Gin Ling Way, Old Chinatown Plaza; Tel. (213) 687-9905*); **Flock Shop** (*943 N Broadway at Bernard, #103; Tel. (213) 229-9090*); **Ooga Booga** (*943 N Broadway at Bernard, #203; Tel. (213) 617-1105*).

The Los Angeles Flower Market (**A** C5)
→ *754 Wall St (8th) Mon-Sat 8am (6am Tue, Thu, Sat)–noon*
The nation's largest market for wholesale flowers. The general public can enjoy this visual and fragrant spectacle for a minimal entrance fee: $2 ($1 Sat).

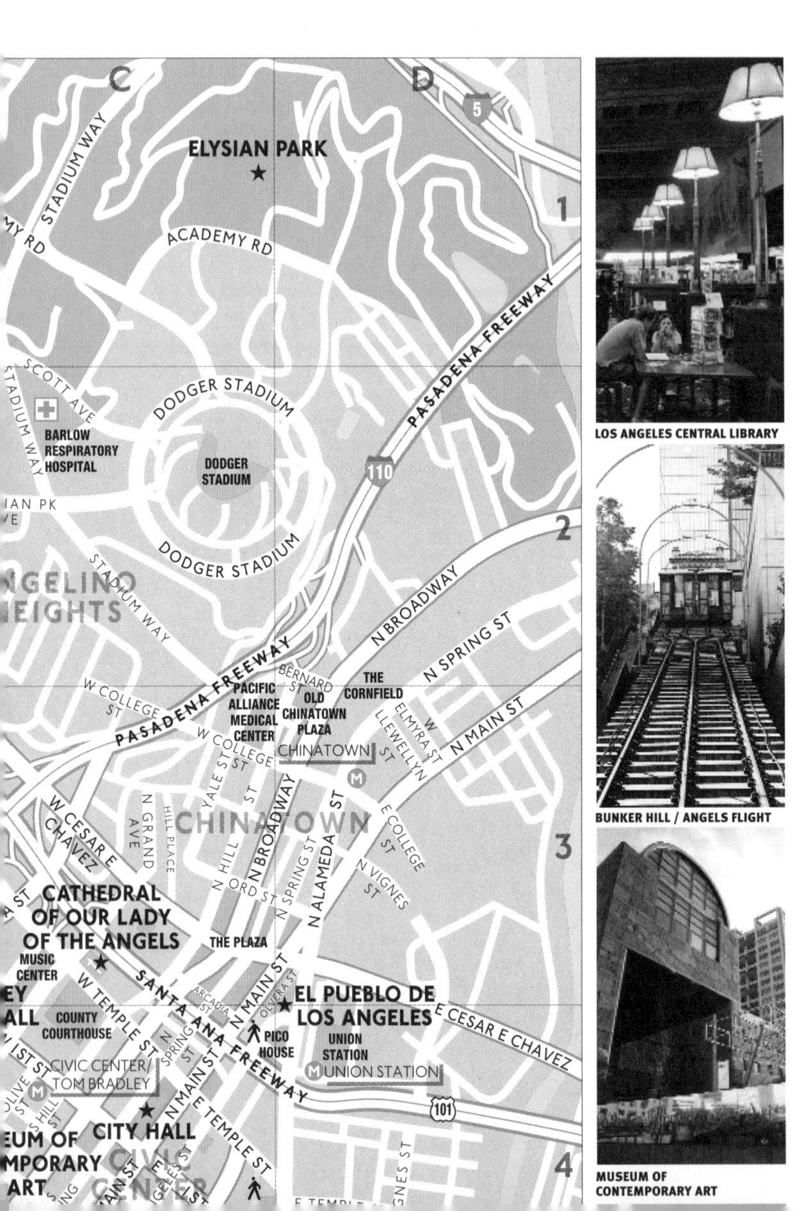

LOS ANGELES CENTRAL LIBRARY

BUNKER HILL / ANGELS FLIGHT

MUSEUM OF CONTEMPORARY ART

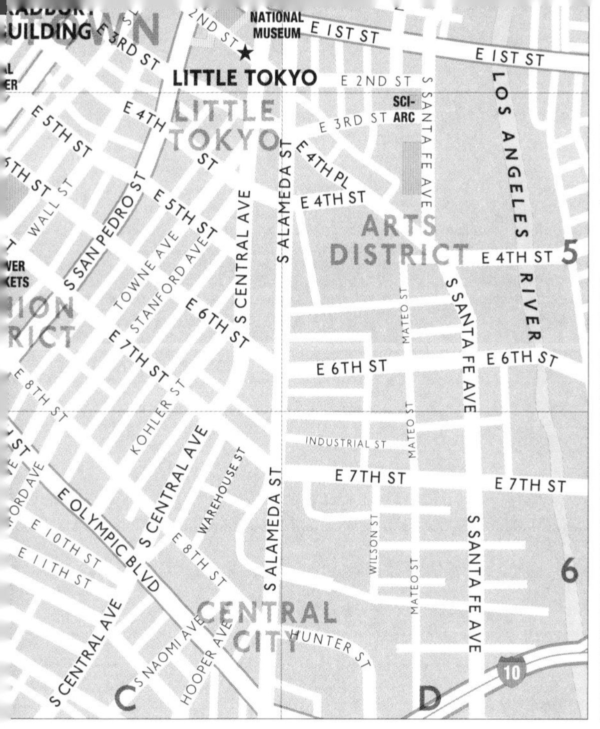

WALT DISNEY CONCERT HALL

CATHEDRAL OF OUR LADY OF THE ANGELS

(213) 228-7000; Mon-Sat ·m–8pm (6pm Fri-Sat); ı 1–5pm; at least one k-in tour offered daily
dernist elements as well a new wing were added ɛr two devastating fires .986, as part of the ensive renovation, but most impressive ;ment is the second-floor ında with a dozen rals depicting the history :alifornia.

Bunker Hill (**A** B4)
; once elegant neighbor- ›d fell into ruin by the os, leaving an urban ıeau that would inspire likes of Raymond ndler and Charles Bukowski. High-rises and stylized plazas have since replaced the dilapidated Victorian manses. While Angels Flight, known as the World's Shortest Funicular, remains inoperative, one can reach the top of the hill using the Bunker Hill Steps.

★ **Museum of Contemporary Art** (**A** C4)
→ 250 S Grand Ave (2nd)
Tel. (213) 621-1745
Thu 11am–8pm; Fri-Mon 11am–5pm (6pm Sat-Sun)
The distinctive redstone building perched atop Bunker Hill is the flagship of the museum's three facilities. MOCA was created in 1979 and is dedicated to art of the last 70 years. The permanent collection boasts the works of such masters as Jackson Pollock, Diane Arbus, Robert Rauschenberg and David Hockney.

★ **Walt Disney Concert Hall** (**A** C4)
→ 111 S Grand Ave (1st)
Tel. (213) 972-7211; Check tour schedule for start times; www.disneyhall.org
Frank Gehry's leviathan of undulating steel is the latest addition to the Music Center complex (2003). In its superior acoustics and a terraced 2,265-seat arrangement that encircles the stage, it is designed to elevate the sense of intimacy between audience and performer. While the public is invited to explore the building during the day – self-guided and docent tours are complimentary – the auditorium is off-limits.

★ **Cathedral of Our Lady of the Angels** (**A** C3)
→ 555 W Temple St (Grand)
Mon-Fri 6.30am–6pm; Sat 9am–6pm; Sun 7am–6pm
The postmodern lines and angles of this sprawling, 11-story-high edifice (Rafael Moneo, 2002) loom over the 101 Freeway with L.A. sculptor Robert Graham's magnificently engraved Great Bronze Doors.

CHURCH OF SCIENTOLOGY
LONGPREE AVE
FOUNTAIN AVE
LITTLE ARMENIA
HOLLYWOOD FREEWAY
LEXINGTON AVE
SANTA MONICA BLVD
HOLLYWOOD FOREVER CEMETERY
4
PARAMOUNT STUDIOS
ROMAINE ST
MONROE ST
LEMON GROVE AVE
VERMONT/ SANTA MONICA/ L.A. CITY COLLEGE
L.A. CITY COLLEGE
N BRONSON AVE
N VAN NESS AVE
N WILTON PL
N ST ANDREWS
N RIDGEWOOD PL
N WESTERN AVE
N OXFORD AVE
N SERRANO AVE
N HOBART BLVD
N KINGSLEY DRIVE
N ARDMORE AVE
N NORMANDIE AVE
N MARIPOSA AVE
N ALEXANDRIA AVE
N KENMORE AVE
HELIOTROPE DR
N BERENDO ST
N NEW HAMPSHIRE AVE
NORTH VERMONT AVE
101
MELROSE AVE
A
B
C

HOLLYHOCK HOUSE

SILVER LAKE RESERVOIR

★ **Hollywood Sign** (off **B** A1)
→ *Not open to the public; the best views can be had at the end of Beachwood Drive or from Griffith Observatory*
Originally an advertisement for a housing development, the sign read 'Hollywoodland' at the time of its dedication in 1923. A $90,000 surveillance system was installed in 1994 to ensure its protection.

★ **Griffith Park** (**B** A-E1)
→ *4730 Crystal Springs Drive Daily 5am–10.30pm (trails close at sunset)*
The more than 4,210 acres of land, which extend along the eastern side of the Santa Monica mountains, were a Christmas gift from Griffith J. Griffith to the city of Los Angeles in 1896. Among its many attractions are hiking trails, camping and picnic areas, two museums, a merry-go-round and the Los Angeles Zoo.

★ **Observatory** (**B** B1-2)
→ *2800 E Observatory Rd Tel. (213) 473-0800; Tue-Sun noon (10am Sat-Sun)–10pm*
Griffith's will left bequests for this recently restored 1935 Art Deco observatory. The original Zeiss telescope is used mainly for nighttime viewings. Featured in the film *Rebel Without a Cause*, it offers matchless vistas of the L.A. Basin.

★ **Greek Theatre** (**B** C1)
→ *2700 N Vermont Ave Tel. (323) 665-5857; Box office hours: Mon-Fri noon–6pm; Sat-Sun 10am–4pm; www.greektheatrela.com*
This 5,870-seat outdoor theater built in 1929 has a stage modeled after an ancient Greek temple, complete with pediment, and remarkable acoustics. Numerous artists have performed here, including David Bowie, Sting, The Who and Al Green.

★ **Barnsdall Art Park** (**B** C3)
→ *4800 Hollywood Blvd Daily 5am–10.30pm; the Municipal Art Gallery, Art Center and Gallery Theatre each keep their own hours info available online: www.barnsdallartpark.cor*
Oil heiress Aline Barnsc donated this former oliv grove to the city in 1927 Today as a public park i hosts art classes, exhibitions, museum tc theater programs, festiv and other cultural even

★ **Hollyhock House** (**B** C3)
→ *4800 Hollywood Blvd Tel. (323) 644-6269; Tours*

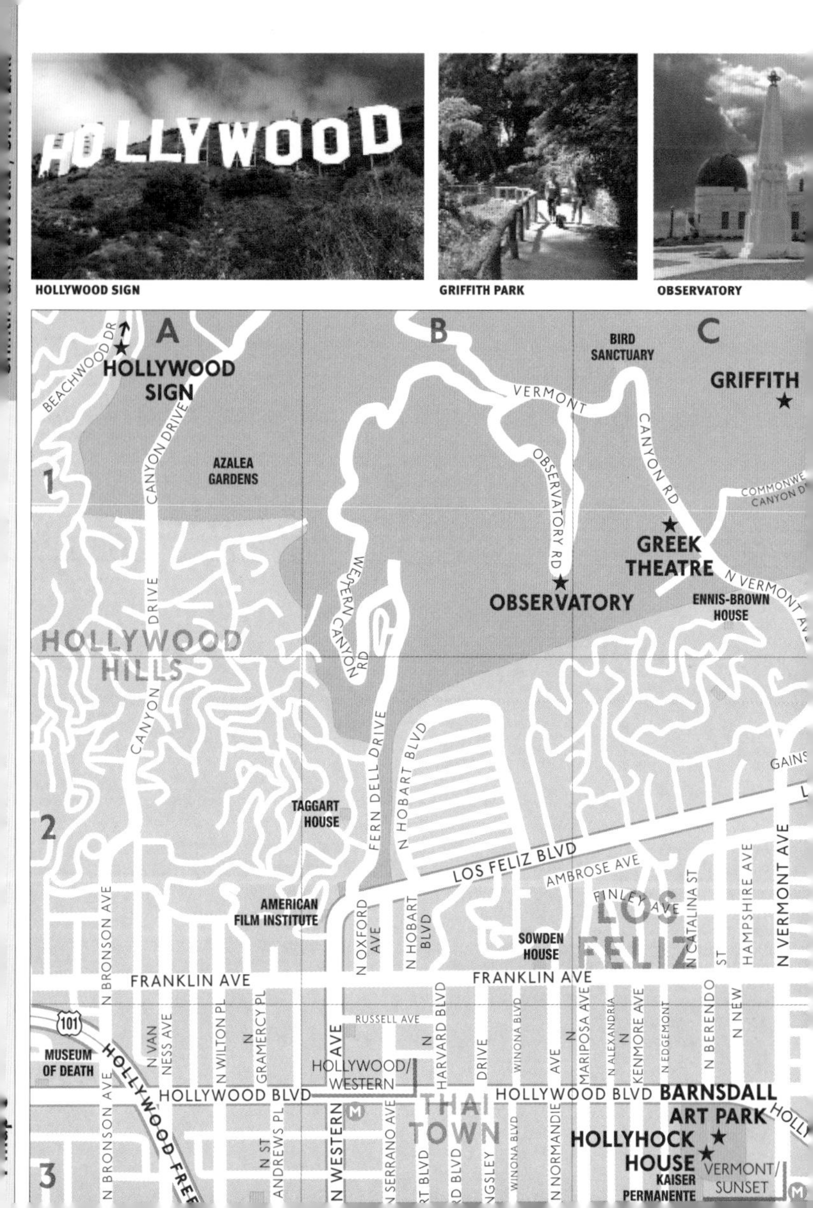

HOLLYWOOD SIGN

GRIFFITH PARK

OBSERVATORY

Just south of the Santa Monica mountains, the wedge of land between Downtown and Griffith Park is reductively known as the 'Eastside' (there's a lot more left of L.A. heading eastward). This is also indie territory defined by the hipster counterculture of artists and struggling screenwriters, musicians and club kids. A bohemian gentrification has set up coffeehouses and yoga studios among the taco shacks and auto shops. This is also the Los Angeles of Frank Lloyd Wright and Richard Neutra, whose legacy can be seen in the modernist manses that enrich the surrounding hills.

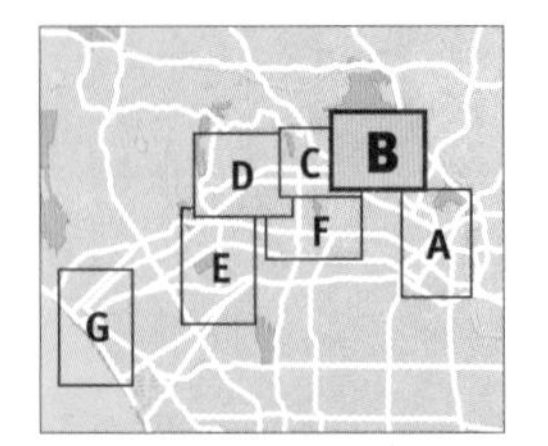

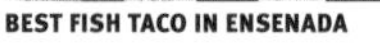
BEST FISH TACO IN ENSENADA

SQUARE ONE

RESTAURANTS

Best Fish Taco in Ensenada (**B** D3)
→ *1650 Hillhurst Ave (Prospect); Daily 11am–8pm (or when tacos run out)*
This wee shack takes its big name seriously: the Baja-style fish taco is – aside from a shrimp option – the only menu item; each is topped with homemade salsa, crema, and then served, one at a time. Cash only. $2.

Yuca's (**B** D2)
→ *2056 Hillhurst Ave (Ambrose); Tel. (323) 662-1214; Mon-Sat 11am–6pm*
Cochinita pibil, Yucatan-style slow-roasted pork, offered as a burrito, taco or torta sets this family-owned institution apart. Yucatecan tamales are a popular Saturday-only specialty. $4.

Square One Dining (**B** C4)
→ *4854 Fountain Ave (Catalina); Tel. (323) 661-1109; Daily 8am–3pm*
Breakfast here is an elegant, all-day affair with organic, locally sourced produce. Try the brioche French toast topped with banana-citrus caramel or baked eggs with braised greens and Gruyère. Delicious hot and cold sandwiches. $10.

Little Dom's (**B** D2)
→ *2128 Hillhurst Ave (Los Feliz); Tel. (323) 661-0055 Daily 8am–3pm, 6–11pm (midnight Fri-Sat)*
Pictures of 1930s and '40s Hollywood stars hang above the red leather booths of this vintage-seeming spot. Spaghetti and meatballs and arancini are delicious classics, but the forward-thinking kitchen also uses seasonal ingredients and throws fennel pollen in to the Béarnaise sauce. A to-go deli counter is a recent addition. $15.

Alcove Cafe & Bakery (**B** D2)
→ *1929 Hillhurst Ave (Franklin); Tel. (323) 644-0100; Daily 6am (7am Sun)–11pm*
This charming local hangout typifies the laid-back, arty spirit of Los Feliz – despite the more than occasional celebrity or two. Alfresco dining on the brick patio is a must. Excellent desserts. $13.

Café Stella (**B** D4)
→ *3932 W Sunset Blvd (Hyperion)*
Tel. (323) 666-0265; Daily 6–11pm (10pm Sun)
One of the best-kept secrets of Silver Lake, this

TTLE DOM'S

DRESDEN ROOM

WACKO

hip French bistro has a classic menu with excellent charcuterie to start, delicious lamb chops or steak frites, and tapenade or chevre for your baguette; you can eat outside, too, among oleander, lavender and potted olive trees. $18–25.

CAFÉS, ICE-CREAM PARLORS

L.A. Mill Coffee Boutique (**B** E4)
→ *1636 Silver Lake Blvd (Effie) Tel. (323) 663-4441; Daily 7am–10am (11pm Fri-Sat)*
From the baroque chandelier and imported French wallpaper to the meticulous extraction methods, this is the ultimate brew shop, but breakfast, lunch and dinner are equally highbrow.

Casbah Café (**B** D4)
→ *3900 W Sunset Blvd (Hyperion); Tel. (323) 664-7000; Daily 6am–11pm*
A great place to get tea or coffee, a sandwich, mushroom frittata or cookies and relax against a brocade pillow and dream of North Africa.

Scoops (**B** C4)
→ *712 Heliotrope Dr. (Melrose); Tel. (323) 906-2649; Mon-Sat noon–10pm; Sun 2–6pm*
Unorthodox inventions like bacon caramel, foie gras onion, and blackberry balsamic vinegar have garnered a cult following. Flavors, which always include several vegan options, change daily.

PUBS, BARS, MUSIC VENUES

Pure Luck (**B** C4)
→ *707 N Heliotrope Dr. (Melrose) Tel. (323) 660-5993 Mon-Sat 11am–midnight*
A brew pub with a vegan menu, its popularity extends well beyond herbivores. Impressive selection of craftsman beers at around $5 a pint only.

Edendale Grill (**B** F2)
→ *2838 Rowena Ave (Auburn); Tel. (323) 666-2000; Daily 5pm–midnight (2am Thu-Sat)*
This 1924 former fire station has tin ceilings and dark wood. Have a drink outside and, if you get hungry, *moules frites* and roasted chicken are great.

Cha Cha Lounge (**B** F3)
→ *2375 Glendale Blvd (Silver Lake); Tel. (323) 660-7595 Daily 5pm–2am*
This tiki-themed watering hole serves up flamboyant decor and enormous tropical cocktails for the eminently hip. Foosball tables and a photo booth round out the fun.

The Dresden Room (**B** C3)
→ *1760 N Vermont Ave (Melbourne); Tel. (323) 665-4294; Daily 4.30–11pm (10pm Sun)*
Also a restaurant, but the real draw is jazz crooners Marty and Elayne, who have commanded the piano bar since 1982. An evening at the Dresden was famously captured in the movie *Swingers*.

Spaceland (**B** F4)
→ *1717 Silver Lake Blvd (Effie); Tel. (323) 661-4380*
The first show in 1995 featured yet-unknowns Beck and a newly formed band called the Foo Fighters. Since then, the club has anchored Eastside's incredibly dynamic indie rock scene. Mondays are free nights dedicated to new talent.

SHOPPING

Wacko (**B** C3)
→ *4633 Hollywood Blvd (Rodney); Tel. (323) 663-0122 Mon-Sat 11am–7pm (9pm Thu-Sat); Sun noon–6pm*
A psychedelic façade and, inside, retro cartoon memorabilia, incense, robots, skeletons, tiki gear, *luchador* masks, books and cards with an R-rated twist. At the back of the store is the La Luz de Jesus art gallery.

Cake Jewelry (**B** C3)
→ *4649 Russell Ave (Vermont); Tel. (323) 644-5699; Mon-Sat 11am–6pm; Sun noon–5pm*
Gold, sterling and semiprecious stones are hand-forged locally; also emerging designers.

Skylight Books (**B** C3)
→ *1818 N Vermont Ave (Franklin); Tel. (323) 660-1175; Daily 10am–10pm*
One of L.A.'s best and most beloved independent bookstores, it has an encyclopedic selection. Employees are particularly literate.

Confederacy (**B** C3)
→ *4661 Hollywood Blvd (Vermont); Tel. (323) 913-3040 Daily 11am–8pm (7pm Sun)*
This fantastic 5,000-sq.-ft space – named after the book *A Confederacy of Dunces* – with 16-ft ceilings, brick walls, tin and wood-beam ceilings, has women's and men's clothing, accessories, gifts, books, perfumes and even a gallery area for new artists.

GREEK THEATRE
BARNSDALL ART PARK / MUNICIPAL ART GALLERY
D
E
F
1
2
3
AUTRY NATIONAL CENTER OF THE AMERICAN WEST
PONY AND TRAIN RIDES
VISTA DEL VALLE
CRYSTAL SPRING DR
GRIFFITH PARK DR
LOS FELIZ BLVD
ATWATER VILLAGE
GLENDALE BLVD
GARDEN AVE
HOLLYDALE DRIVE
WALT DISNEY HOUSE
N COMMONWEALTH AVE
CROMWELL AVE
GRIFFITH PARK BLVD
RIVERSIDE DRIVE
GOLDEN STATE FREEWAY
LOS ANGELES RIVER
WAVERLY DRIVE
LOWRY RD
ROWENA AVE
ROWENA RESERVOIR
HYPERION AVE
PRICE
FINLEY AVE
CLARISSA AVE
HILLHURST AVE
TALMADGE ST
MYRA AVE
ST GEORGE ST
AUBURN ST
W SILVER LAKE DR
ANKLIN AVE
RUSSELL AVE
SHAKESPEARE BRIDGE
ABC TELEVISION CENTER
FRANKLIN AVE
MICHELTORENA ST
MORENO DRIVE
KENILWORTH AVE
ARMSTRONG AVE
IVANHOE RESERVOIR
SILVER LAKE
PROSPECT AVE
CAMERO AVE
CLAYTON AVE
CUMBERLAND AVE
ROSALIA RD
SILVER LAKE RESERVOIR
EDGEWATER TERRACE
BRIER AVE
DEANE ST

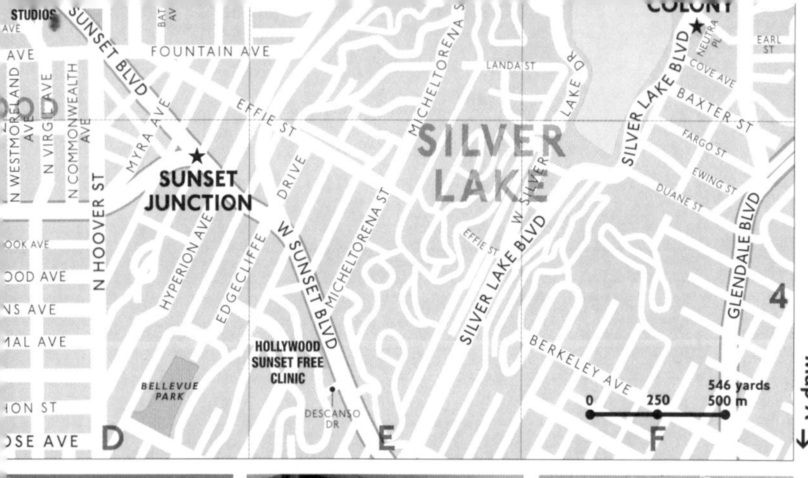

NSET JUNCTION

NEUTRA COLONY

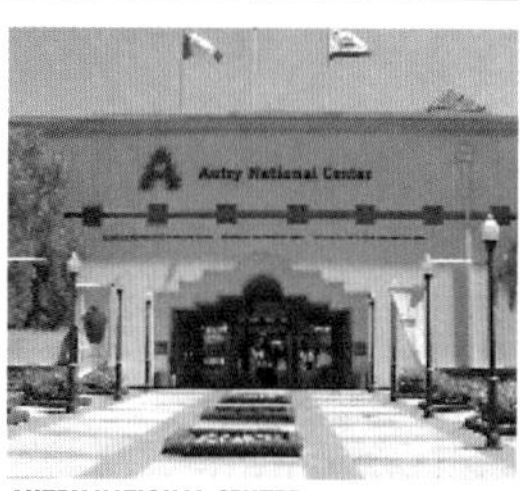

AUTRY NATIONAL CENTER

ery hour on the half hour, ed-Sun 12.30–3.30pm
1921 Frank Lloyd Wright signed this Mayan-luenced residence – his st of many projects in the y – for Aline Barnsdall in style he referred to as alifornia Romanza'; it is med for the owner's orite flower, used as a tif throughout.

Silver Lake servoir (**B** F3)
Along Silver Lake Blvd and Silver Lake Dr.
sides providing water the city, Silver Lake and neighboring Ivanhoe servoir are a serene ckdrop for the popular jogging path that winds around them. The southern edge of the 127-acre site adjoins a dog park and a recreation center.

★ Sunset Junction (**B** D4)
→ *Santa Monica Blvd and W Sunset Blvd*
The site of an old railcar junction, in 1967 this intersection of two of L.A.'s largest thoroughfares witnessed the early gay-rights Black Cat protest against police discrimination. The enclave of trendy cafés, restaurants and boutiques has kept much of its bohemian identity. The annual summer street fair in August has become a destination event featuring an all-star music lineup.

★ Neutra Colony (**B** F3)
→ *Neutra Place (Earl)*
The pioneering modern architect Richard Neutra (1892–1970) designed the glass houses that can be seen from the street on and around Neutra Place. Neutra's son and partner, Dion, carries on the family business from his nearby studio, the Neutra Institute. Other Neutra buildings in the neighborhood include the VDL House II (*2300 Silver Lake Blvd at Deane*), which is occasionally available for touring, and the old Neutra Office Building (*2379 Glendale Blvd at Brier*).

★ Autry National Center of the American West (off **B** E1)
→ *4700 Western Heritage Way Tel. (323) 667-2000; Tue-Fri 10am–4pm; Sat-Sun 11am–5pm*
The cornerstone of the center, dedicated to the study of the American West, is the Museum of the American West, founded by movie star cowboy Gene Autry, and located in the northern sector of Griffith Park. Aside from collections of guns, baskets and other artifacts, special exhibitions have also celebrated rockabilly and the Westerns of Sergio Leone.

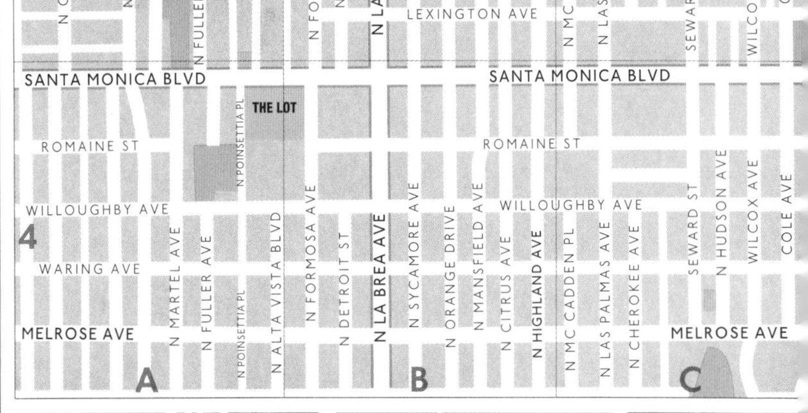

WALK OF FAME

CAPITOL RECORDS BUILDING

ROOSEVELT HOTEL

★ **Universal Studios / CityWalk** (off **C** C1)
→ *100 Universal City Plaza (Lankershim); Tel. (800) UNIVERSAL; hours for park & CityWalk vary: www.universalstudioshollywood.com*
The popular studio tour drives through famous movie and television sets: see the Bates Motel from *Psycho*, Wisteria Lane from *Desparate Housewives* and experience an earthquake. For more frightening fun there are the pyrotechnics of the *Backdraft* ride, and the dinosaurs and 80-ft water plunge of *Jurassic Park*. The adjacent CityWalk has a movie theater with an eight-story IMAX screen, restaurants, bars and shops.

★ **Runyon Canyon** (**C** A1)
→ *1865 N Fuller Ave (Franklin); Daily dawn to dusk*
The city's fittest citizens gather here mornings and afternoons to hike the trails and do yoga, and dogs are allowed off-leash. The views are excellent.

★ **Hollywood Bowl** (**C** B1)
→ *2301 N Highland Ave (Odin); Tel. (323) 436-2827 Concerts: late spring to fall*
The summer home of the Los Angeles Philharmonic, 'the Bowl' is a natural amphitheater and one of the largest in the world. This fair-weather venue has hosted such celebrated musicians as the Beatles, Leonard Bernstein and Pavarotti. The annual Fourth of July Fireworks Spectacular is the most sought-after ticket.

★ **Grauman's Egyptian Theatre** (**C** C2)
→ *6712 Hollywood Blvd (Las Palmas); Tel. (323) 461-2020*
The complex, with its massive columns and palm tree- and hieroglyphic-decorated courtyard, was built in 1922 at the height of American Egypt-mania. The red-carpet movie premiere began here with the opening of Douglas Fairbanks's *Robin Hood* the same year. Like its young sibling below, the venue still a fully operational movie house.

★ **Grauman's Chinese Theatre** (**C** B2)
→ *6801 Hollywood Blvd (Orange); Tel. (323) 464-81*
Perhaps the world's mos famous movie palace, it built in 1927 for $2 millic with parts brought in fro China. Over 200 Hollywc personalities (and their various body parts) have been immortalized in th pavement.

★ **Walk of Fame** (**C** B-
→ *Hollywood Blvd (betwe Gower and La Brea) and V St (between Yucca and Su*

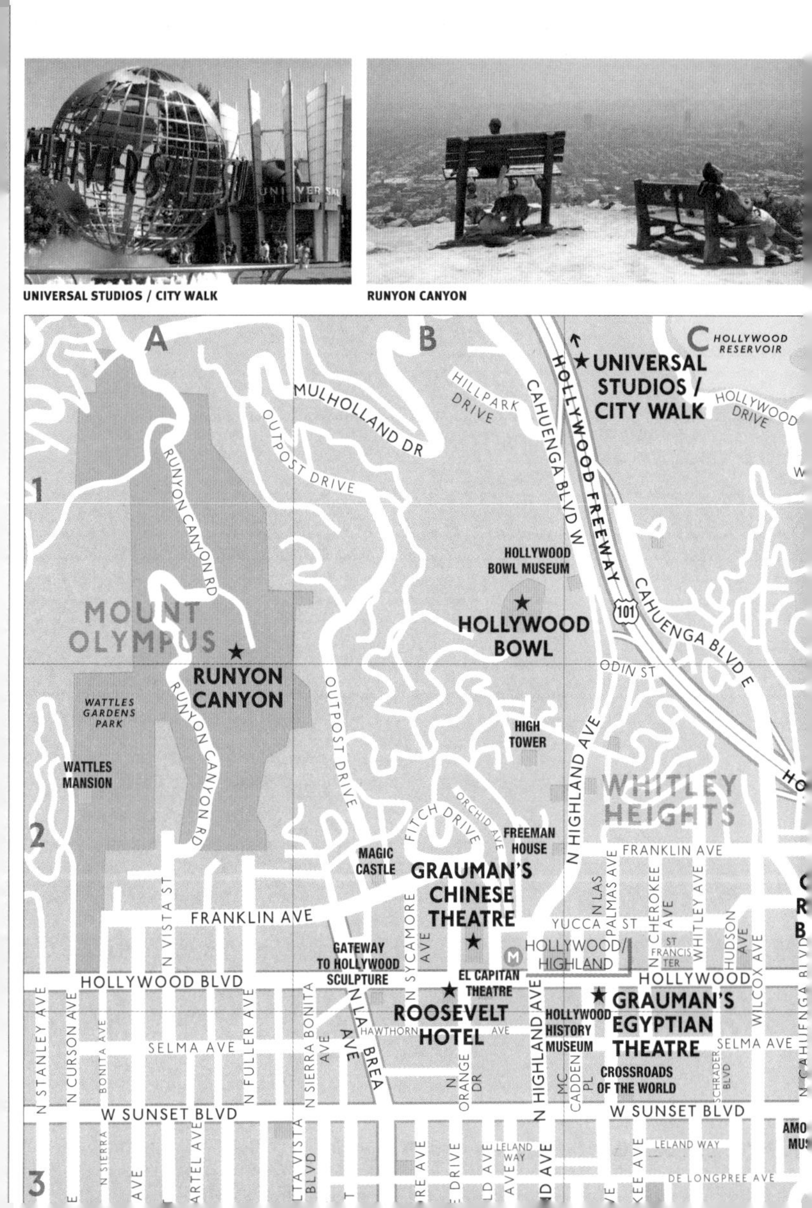
UNIVERSAL STUDIOS / CITY WALK
RUNYON CANYON
A
B
C
HOLLYWOOD RESERVOIR
UNIVERSAL STUDIOS / CITY WALK
HILLPARK DRIVE
HOLLYWOOD DRIVE
MULHOLLAND DR
OUTPOST DRIVE
CAHUENGA BLVD W
HOLLYWOOD FREEWAY
101
CAHUENGA BLVD E
RUNYON CANYON RD
HOLLYWOOD BOWL MUSEUM
HOLLYWOOD BOWL
MOUNT OLYMPUS
RUNYON CANYON
ODIN ST
WATTLES GARDENS PARK
WATTLES MANSION
HIGH TOWER
N HIGHLAND AVE
WHITLEY HEIGHTS
FITCH DRIVE
ORCHID AVE
FREEMAN HOUSE
MAGIC CASTLE
GRAUMAN'S CHINESE THEATRE
FRANKLIN AVE
N VISTA ST
N SYCAMORE AVE
YUCCA ST
N LAS PALMAS AVE
N CHEROKEE AVE
WHITLEY AVE
HUDSON AVE
WILCOX AVE
ST FRANCIS TER
HOLLYWOOD/HIGHLAND
GATEWAY TO HOLLYWOOD SCULPTURE
EL CAPITAN THEATRE
HOLLYWOOD BLVD
ROOSEVELT HOTEL
HOLLYWOOD HISTORY MUSEUM
GRAUMAN'S EGYPTIAN THEATRE
N STANLEY AVE
N CURSON AVE
BONITA AVE
SELMA AVE
N FULLER AVE
N SIERRA BONITA AVE
N LA BREA AVE
HAWTHORN AVE
N ORANGE DR
MC CADDEN PL
CROSSROADS OF THE WORLD
SCHRADER BLVD
N CAHUENGA BLVD
W SUNSET BLVD
LELAND WAY
DE LONGPREE AVE
N SIERRA
1
2
3

Some studios decamped to the valley, and tattoo parlors, strip clubs and souvenir shops flooded the boulevards. Yet, the indelible symbols of Hollywood's Golden era still remain. As with the rest of Los Angeles, revitalization is the key word of late, starting with a multimillion-dollar nightlife scene built on velvet ropes and the imprudence of young celebrities. Flashy real estate enterprises like the condominiums of the W Hotel Hollywood are looking to attract a residential community. And the movie industry has returned to roost in the annual Oscars ceremony at the Kodak Theatre.

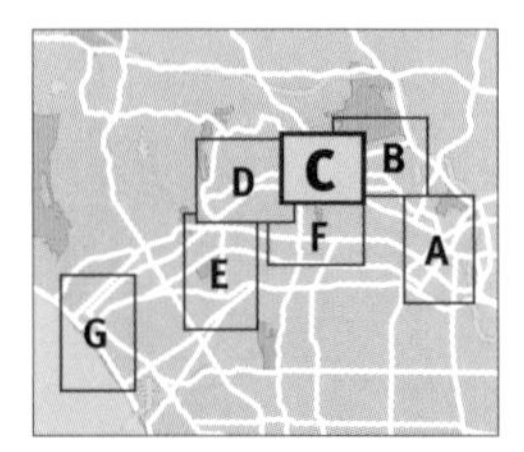

THAI TOWN

KATSUYA

RESTAURANTS

In-N-Out Burger (**C** B3)
→ *7009 W Sunset Blvd (La Brea); Tel. (800) 786-1000*
Daily 10.30am–1am
This hugely popular chain offers hamburgers, cheeseburgers, Double-Doubles and French fries, with a soda or a shake; beef is free of additives and preservatives. This is where everyone goes after the ceremony on Academy Award night. Meal $6.

Pink's Hot Dog (**C** B4)
→ *709 N La Brea Ave (Melrose); Tel. (323) 931-4223; Daily 9.30am–2am (3am Fri-Sat)*
This started as a pushcart in 1939. The all-beef dogs come with a dizzying choice of toppings, including chili. $5.

Thai Town (**C** F2)
→ *Hollywood Blvd, between Western and Normandie*
Sanamluang Cafe (*5170 Hollywood Blvd at Kingsley, Tel. (323) 660-8006,* **C** F2) and **Sapp Coffee Shop** (*5183 Hollywood Blvd at Kingsley, Tel. (323) 665-1035,* **C** F2) are favored for the noodle dishes; **Jitlada's** Southern Thai specialties (*5233 W Sunset Blvd at Harvard, Tel. (323) 663-3104,* **C** F3) are easily the spiciest offerings on the strip. Most take cash only.

The Hungry Cat (**C** D3)
→ *1535 Vine St (Sunset)*
Tel. (323) 462-2155
Mon-Sat noon–midnight (11pm Mon-Wed); Sun 11am–11pm
This sleek, casual creation of master chef Suzanne Goin and her husband, David Lentz, draws on organic produce to create a brilliant menu. There is a raw-bar menu and such dishes as fish sandwich with heirloom tomatoes or Pug burger with bacon, avocado and blue cheese for lunch, and clams with chorizo for dinner. $15–25.

Katsuya (**C** D2)
→ *6300 Hollywood Blvd (Vine); Tel. (323) 871-8777*
Mon-Fri 11.30am–2pm, 5.30pm–midnight (11pm Mon); Sat 5.30pm–12.30am; Sun 4–11pm
The collaboration – one of four in the city – between sushi master Katsuya Uechi, designer Philippe Starck and entrepreneurial nightlife company SBE draws a scene more inclined toward saketinis than sashimi. $18.

Ammo (**C** B3)
→ *1155 N Highland Ave (Lexington); Tel. (323) 871-2666; Mon-Fri 11.30am–2.30pm, 6–10pm (11pm Fri); Sat 5.30–11pm; Sun 5–9pm*

JSSO & FRANK GRILL

AMOEBA MUSIC

CINERAMA DOME

Chef Amy Sweeney cooks up organic, seasonal produce, and aside from thin-crust pizzas there are such dishes as risotto verde with zucchini, squash blossoms and asparagus, braised bass with baby artichokes, or grilled Nimen Ranch hanger steak. Low-key, cool and favored by industry types. $24.

Musso & Frank Grill (**C** C2)
→ *6667 Hollywood Blvd (Cherokee); Tel. (323) 467-7788; Tue-Sat 11am–11pm*
This storied steakhouse used to comfort the likes of Dashiell Hammett, F. Scott Fitzgerald and Dorothy Parker. Steaks with stiff martinis can still be had in a red leather booth or at the mahogany counter. $25.

BARS, MOVIE HOUSES, THEATERS, MUSIC VENUES

The Cat & Fiddle (**C** C3)
→ *6530 W Sunset Blvd (Schrader); Tel. (323) 468-3800; Daily 11.30am–2am*
The lovely patio appeals to lunching industry types as much as the after-hours crowd who lounge about the Spanish-style fountain.

Teddy's (**C** B2)
→ *7000 Hollywood Blvd (Orange); Tel. (323) 466-7000; Fri-Sat, Mon 10pm–2am*
Ensconced in the Roosevelt Hotel, this bar-lounge is seductively dark and cavelike – unsurprisingly, a den of celebrity ubiquity.

ArcLight Hollywood / Cinerama Dome (**C** C3)
→ *6360 W Sunset Blvd (Ivar) Tel. (323) 464-1478 www.arclightcinemas.com*
The 14-screen complex features the first – and one of the last remaining – Cinerama Domes, now restored, in the world. The 1963 geodesic structure is a stellar place to experience the sights and sounds of movie magic.

The Pantages Theater (**C** D2)
→ *6233 Hollywood Blvd (Vine); Tel. (323) 468-1700 www.pantages-theater.com*
This 1939 landmark theater was once a movie palace – the gilded Art Deco design now sets the stage for such musical productions as *The Lion King*, *The Producers* and *Wicked*.

The Groundlings (**C** A4)
→ *7307 Melrose Ave (Poinsettia); Tel. (323) 934-4747; Shows Wed-Sat 8pm (plus 10pm Fri-Sat); 7.30pm Sun; www.groundlings.com*
This improv troupe claims the most illustrious alumni: Will Ferrell, Lisa Kudrow, Jon Lovitz; even Paul Reubens and his signature Pee Wee Herman character got their comedic feet wet here.

Hollywood Palladium (**C** D3)
→ *6215 W Sunset Blvd (Argyle); Tel. (323) 962-7600 www.livenation.com*
Now renovated, this historic Art Deco venue, which had debuted in 1940 with Frank Sinatra and the Tommy Dorsey Orchestra, had Rapper Jay-Z christen the improved staging and acoustics at the much-heralded 2008 reopening.

SHOPPING

Hollywood & Highland (**C** B2)
→ *6801 Hollywood Blvd (Highland); Daily 10am–10pm (7pm Sun)*
This is the city's most flamboyant mall with its neon- and billboard-covered façade and a courtyard filled with Babylonian reliefs and giant elephants atop columns. The property also includes the Kodak Theatre, home of the Oscars ceremony.

Amoeba Music (**C** C3)
→ *6400 Sunset Blvd (Ivar) Tel. (323) 245-6400 Mon-Sat 10.30am–11pm; Sun 11am–9pm*
A wonderland for music lovers, this Berkeley-born transplant carries a whole city block worth of CDs, DVDs, vinyls, both new and used. Practically every genre of music – from jazz and world folk to synthpunk.

Scout (**C** C2)
→ *1646 N Cherokee Ave (Hollywood) Tel. (323) 658-8684; Daily noon–7pm (5pm Sun)*
The boutique showcases vintage pieces as well as the in-house womenswear label that owner Joey Grana designs.

Comic book consumerism
Geeks take heed: **Meltdown** (*7522 W Sunset Blvd at Sierra Bonita, Tel. (323) 851-7223,* **C** A3) is the largest comic-book store on the West Coast. If that isn't enough, another fanboy favorite, **Golden Apple** (*7018 Melrose Ave at La Brea, Tel. (323) 658-6047,* **C** B4), is a mere mile and a half away.

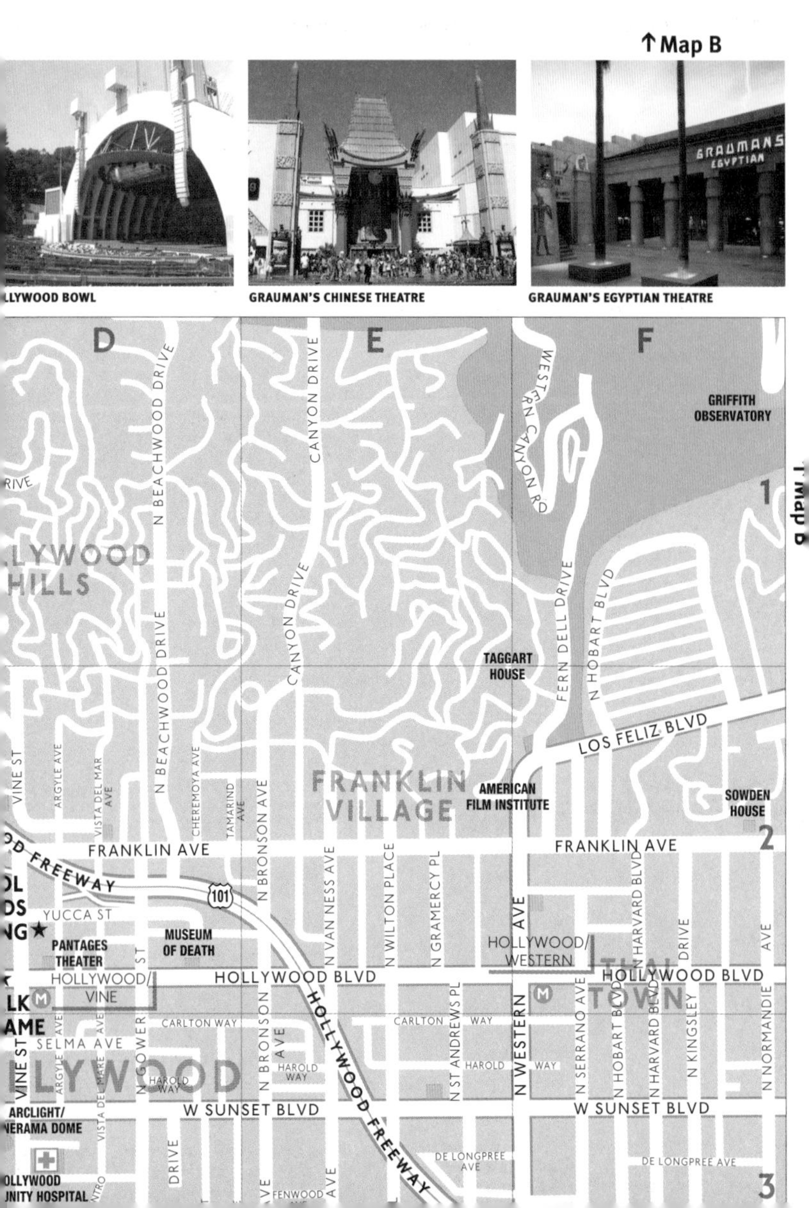

↑Map B
LLYWOOD BOWL
GRAUMAN'S CHINESE THEATRE
GRAUMAN'S EGYPTIAN THEATRE
GRAUMANS EGYPTIAN
D
E
F
1
2
3
GRIFFITH OBSERVATORY
WESTERN CANYON RD
CANYON DRIVE
N BEACHWOOD DRIVE
LYWOOD HILLS
TAGGART HOUSE
FERN DELL DRIVE
N HOBART BLVD
LOS FELIZ BLVD
FRANKLIN VILLAGE
AMERICAN FILM INSTITUTE
SOWDEN HOUSE
FRANKLIN AVE
VINE ST
ARGYLE AVE
VISTA DEL MAR AVE
CHEREMOYA AVE
TAMARIND AVE
N BRONSON AVE
N VAN NESS AVE
N WILTON PLACE
N GRAMERCY PL
HOLLYWOOD FREEWAY
101
YUCCA ST
PANTAGES THEATER
MUSEUM OF DEATH
HOLLYWOOD/ VINE
HOLLYWOOD/ WESTERN
HOLLYWOOD BLVD
THAI TOWN
N HARVARD BLVD
DRIVE
AVE
CARLTON WAY
SELMA AVE
N GOWER ST
HAROLD WAY
N ST ANDREWS PL
N WESTERN AVE
N SERRANO AVE
N KINGSLEY DRIVE
N NORMANDIE AVE
W SUNSET BLVD
ARCLIGHT/ NERAMA DOME
DE LONGPREE AVE
OLLYWOOD UNITY HOSPITAL
FENWOOD

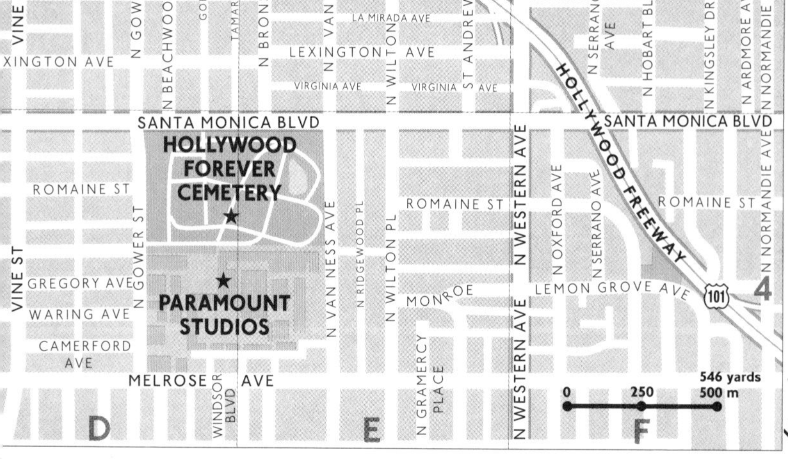

HOLLYWOOD FOREVER CEMETERY

PARAMOUNT STUDIOS

 first pink-terrazzo stars
e included in these
ewalks in 1960 to
nmemorate those who
 contributed to the
ertainment community.
v stars are dedicated all
 time – for a fee of
,000 – giving figures
n movies, music, radio,
and/or theater their due.

**apitol Records
lding** (**C** D2)
*750 Vine St (Yucca)
(323) 462-6252*
 of the city's most
gnizable landmarks,
13-story cylinder apes a
k of vinyl 45s – though
 was not the original
gn intention. There's also a mural entitled *Hollywood Jazz* featuring Miles Davis, Billie Holiday and other legends. The blinking red light on top spells out 'Hollywood' in Morse code.

★ Roosevelt Hotel (**C** B2)
→ *7000 Hollywood Blvd (Orange); Tel. (323) 466-7000*
Now renovated, in the early part of the last century this hotel was a playground for the famous and fabulous. The first Academy Awards ceremony ever was held in the Blossom Room in 1929; the Gable & Lombard Penthouse commemorates two famous residents; David Hockney painted the mural on the floor of the swimming pool.

★ Hollywood Forever Cemetery (**C** D-E4)
→ *6000 Santa Monica Blvd (Van Ness); Tel. (818) 517-5988 (call to inquire about tours)*
Since 1899, this has been the resting place of choice for L.A. elite; Cecil B. DeMille, Bugsy Siegel, and Rudolph Valentino are among dignified crypts and statuary. A walking tour recounts the scandals and mysteries of the Hollywood legends. On Saturday summer nights, classic and cult films are projected onto the side of a mausoleum.

★ Paramount Studios (**C** D-E4)
→ *5555 Melrose Ave (Windsor); Tel. (323) 956-1777 Two-hour tours: Mon-Fri 10am, 11am, 1pm, 2pm*
Only one major movie studio is actually located in Hollywood. Paramount has produced such classic films as *Breakfast at Tiffany's*, *Chinatown*, *The Raiders of the Lost Ark* and its sequels, and *The Godfather trilogy*. The ornate, filigreed gateway was immortalized in *Sunset Boulevard*. Tours take guests through the back lot and include a chance to see filmmaking in action.

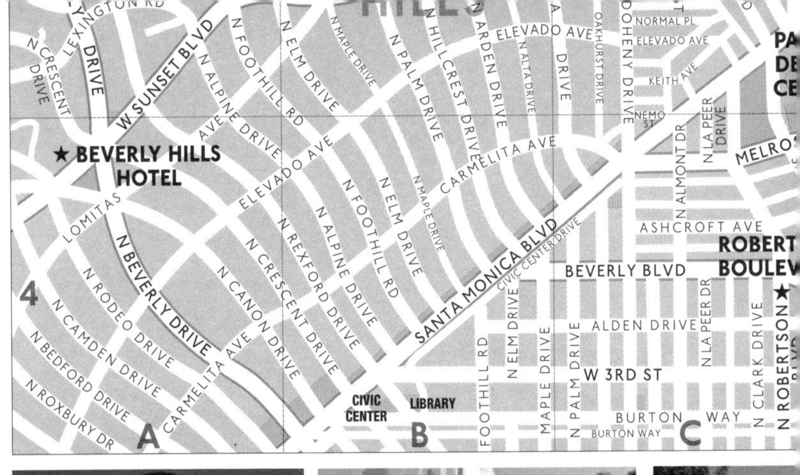

PACIFIC DESIGN CENTER

ROBERTSON BOULEVARD

SCHINDLER HOUSE/MA

★ **Beverly Hills Hotel** (**D** A3)
→ *9641 Sunset Blvd (Crescent); Tel. (310) 276-2251*
This pink landmark, with bungalows set among lush, fragrant gardens, is famous for its vast pool where cabanas can be rented by the day. The Fountain Coffee Room downstairs re-creates a soda counter with its 20 pink stools, and the legendary Polo Lounge is good for celebrity watching at lunchtime.

★ **Greystone Mansion and Park** (**D** B3)
→ *905 Loma Vista Dr. (Robert) Tel. (310) 285-6830 Daily 10am–5pm*
This 1928 Tudor house built for Edward Doheny has 67 rooms and over 18 manicured acres of stables, waterfalls, a greenhouse, tennis courts and pools. It officially became a city park in 1971, and entrance to the grounds is free. *There Will Be Blood* and *Spiderman 3* were recently filmed here.

★ **Sunset Strip** (**D** C3-E2)
→ *Crescent Heights to Doheny*
This glitzy stretch of road got its after-dark reputation in the 1930s, at a time when the area was outside city jurisdiction. Music venues like the Roxy and Whisky a Go Go opened in the 1960s and '70s, establishing the Strip as a destination for the recording industry. Prime real estate is also famously taken up by enormous and provocative billboards.

★ **Chateau Marmont** (**D** E2)
→ *8221 Sunset Blvd (Gordon) Tel. (323) 656-1010*
Renovated by owner Andre Balasz, this hotel was modeled after Château d'Amboise in the Loire Valley, and is a favorite of actors, photographers, and the fashion and music industry. Stories are legion: this was Greta Garbo's hideaway; James Dean climbed through a window after reading *Rebel Witho a Cause*; Jim Belushi and Helmut Newton died her

★ **Stahl House** (**D** D-E
→ *1635 Woods Dr. (Cresce Heights); Tel. (208) 331-14*
Pierre Koenig designed t modernist icon of glass steel in 1959 as but one many Case Study experiments, but 'No. 2 was immortalized in Juli Shulman's famous photograph of the same name. As such, the enduring fantasy of midcentury domesticity also indelibly associate with the emerging Los Angeles that flickered below. Still owned by th

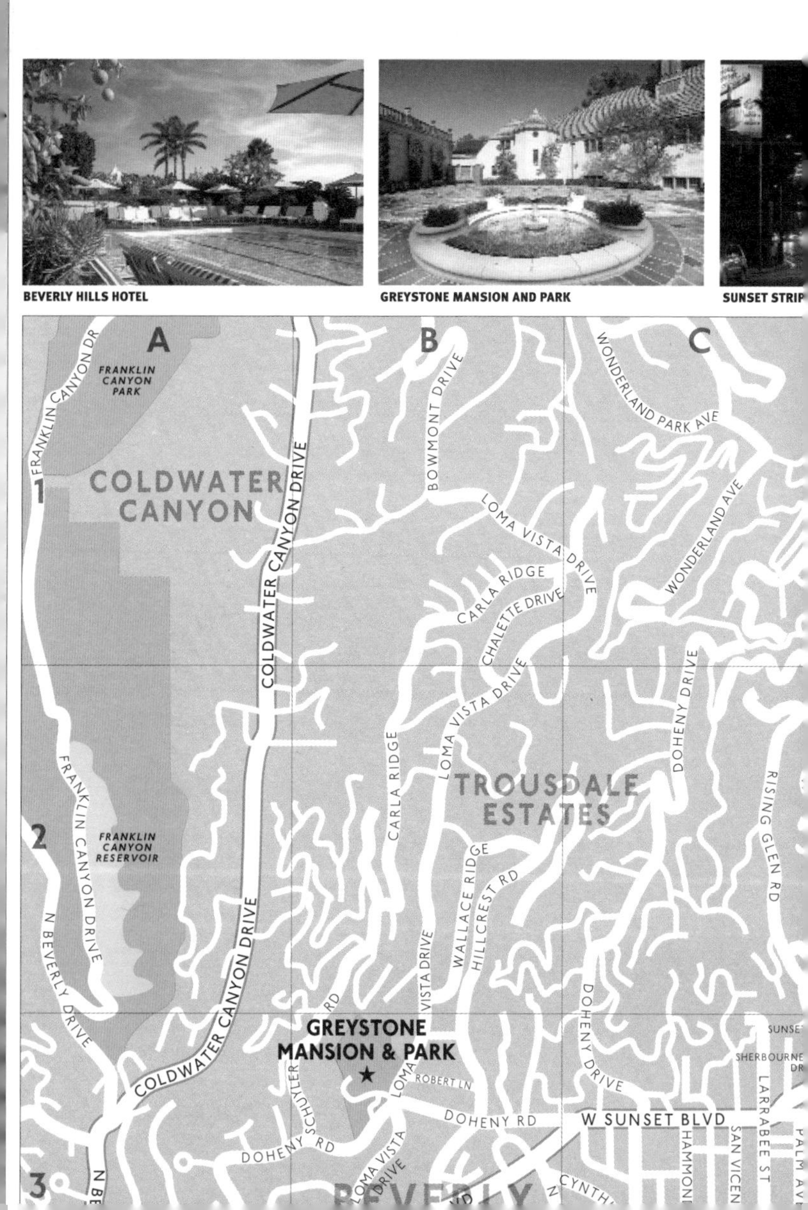
BEVERLY HILLS HOTEL
GREYSTONE MANSION AND PARK
SUNSET STRIP
A
B
C
1
2
3
FRANKLIN CANYON PARK
FRANKLIN CANYON DR
COLDWATER CANYON
COLDWATER CANYON DRIVE
BOWMONT DRIVE
WONDERLAND PARK AVE
WONDERLAND AVE
LOMA VISTA DRIVE
CARLA RIDGE
CHALETTE DRIVE
DOHENY DRIVE
FRANKLIN CANYON DRIVE
FRANKLIN CANYON RESERVOIR
TROUSDALE ESTATES
RISING GLEN RD
WALLACE RIDGE
HILLCREST RD
N BEVERLY DRIVE
VISTA DRIVE
RD
GREYSTONE MANSION & PARK
SCHUYLER
ROBERT LN
DOHENY RD
W SUNSET BLVD
SHERBOURNE DR
LARRABEE ST
SAN VICEN
HAMMONI
PALM AV
CYNTH
N BE

From the gated houses of Doheny Drive to the preserved-in-aspic funk of Laurel Canyon, WeHo is a more youthful, hipper version of Beverly Hills. The rich and famous have made the hills their home while the aspirational rank and file – actors, yuppies, and the like – are in the smaller houses and 1920s Spanish- or château-style apartments of the flats below. Design studios, furniture showrooms and high-fashion boutiques keep company with the Pacific Design Center. Clubs and restaurants line Sunset Strip while rainbow flags decorate Santa Monica Boulevard, announcing the ever-playful predominantly gay community.

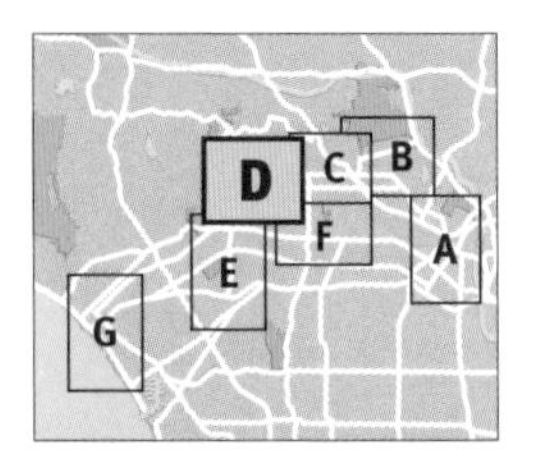

AOC

THE ABBEY

RESTAURANTS

Real Food Daily (**D** D4)
→ *414 N La Cienega Blvd (Oakwood)*
Tel. (310) 289-9910; Mon-Sat 11.30am–10pm (11pm Fri-Sat); Sun 10am–10pm
This organic vegan temple (the original is in Santa Monica) is a favorite among celebrities. $13.

AOC (**D** E4)
→ *8022 W 3rd St (Crescent Heights); Tel. (323) 653-6359 Mon-Fri 6–11pm (10pm Mon); Sat-Sun 5.30–11pm (10pm Sun)*
The small-plates menu is an ideal way to experience the Cal-Mediterranean virtuosity of chef Suzanne Goin. $15.

Cecconi's (**D** C4)
→ *8764 Melrose Ave (Robertson)*
Tel. (310) 432-2000; Mon-Sat 7am–midnight (2am Thu-Sat); Sun 8am–11pm
This Venetian-style restaurant has a northern Italian menu: carpaccios, pizzas, pastas and grilled or wood oven-cooked fish, chicken and meat. On a late night try the midnight menu: everything from quail eggs to tiramisu. $10–24.

Dan Tana's (**D** C4)
→ *9071 Santa Monica Blvd (Nemo); Tel. (310) 275-9444 Daily 5pm–1.30am*
Red-leather booths and an old-fashioned Italian menu of veal scaloppine, spaghetti with meatballs, and steak have made this an institution since 1964. Excellent star watching. $21–54.

The Little Door (**D** E4)
→ *8164 W 3rd St (La Jolla)*
Tel. (323) 951-1210; Daily 6–10.30pm (11.30pm Fri-Sat)
Sample rustic Mediterranean cooking in one of four rooms – among them the patio with koi pond, and the Blue Room with a fireplace and beamed ceiling. Spicy tuna tartare with fennel salad to start or chicken tajine with green olives and zucchini as a main are made from organic, seasonal produce. Try the chocolate truffles on the late-night menu (after 10.30pm). $28–42.

CAFÉS, BARS, CLUBS

3rd Street celebrity brunching (**D** D5)
It's well known that stars come out at brunch on this block, where there is a daily crowd of celebrities, stargazers and paparazzi: **Little Next Door** (*8142 W 3rd St at La Jolla, (323) 951-1010*), **Toast Bakery Cafe**

TLE NEXT DOOR

JOHN VARVATOS

BOOK SOUP

(8221 W 3rd St at Harper, Tel. (323) 655-5018), and **Joan's on Third** (**D** D4)
→ *9350 W Third St (Kings) Tel. (323) 655-2285; Daily 8am–8pm (6pm Sun)*
Aside from catering, this family-owned business now includes a market for baked and gourmet goods, and a café. Try eggs with *pain de mie* for breakfast, and for lunch an apricot-glazed ham-and-Brie sandwich, or tarragon chicken salad; delicious pies, cookies and cupcakes.

Urth Caffe (**D** D3)
→ *8565 Melrose Ave (Westmount); Tel. (310) 659-0628; Daily 6.30am (7am Sat-Sun)–11.30pm*
A steady stream of celebrities and their entourages seek out this organic coffee and tea shop.

The Abbey (**D** C3)
→ *692 N Robertson Blvd (Santa Monica); Tel. (310) 289-8410; Daily 8am–2am*
The cabanas are the most sought-after spots in this ever-popular cavernous space. A gourmet menu rivals the strong drinks. During the day, the Spanish-style courtyard is just as alluring for lunch.

Tower Bar (**D** D2)
→ *8358 Sunset Blvd (Kings) Tel. (323) 654-7100; Mon-Sat 6–10pm (11pm Sat)*
Set in a former Deco apartment building where Bugsy Siegel, Frank Sinatra and Howard Hughes lived, the bar of this restaurant has sweeping views over the city and attracts a West Hollywood and movie crowd.

WeHo club hopping
World-famous acts at these world-famous music venues: **Roxy** (*9009 W Sunset Blvd, Tel. (310) 278-9457*; **D** C3), **Whisky a Go Go** (*8901 Sunset Blvd, Tel. (310) 652-4202*; **D** C3), **Viper Room** (*8852 W Sunset Blvd, Tel. (310) 358-1881*; **D** C3), **House of Blues** (*8430*; **D** C3) *W Sunset Blvd, Tel. (323) 848-5100*), **Troubadour** (*9081 Santa Monica Blvd, Tel. (310) 276-6168*; **D** C4).

SHOPPING

Sunset Plaza (**D** D3)
→ *Sunset Blvd, between Sherbourne and Londonberry*
This two-block strip of high-end boutiques and restaurants lines the boulevard.

Denim Revival (**D** E4)
→ *8044 W 3rd St (Crescent Heights); Tel. (323) 852-0171 Mon-Sat 11am–6pm*
This tailor shop works wonders on worn-out jeans; also an impressive stock of vintage denim and corduroy. Salvaged boots, belts and T-shirts are also in good supply.

Opening Ceremony (**D** D4)
→ *451 N La Cienega Blvd (Rosewood) Tel. (310) 652-1120; Daily 11am (noon Sun)–7pm*
The NYC store opened in the former dance studio of Charlie Chaplin. The 10,000 sq. feet enable designers like Nom de Guerre and Band of Brothers to customize their own retail nooks.

TenOverSix (**D** F4)
→ *7427 Beverly Blvd (Vista) Tel. (323) 330-9355; Mon-Sat 11am–6pm; Sun noon–5pm*
In this avant-garde accessories boutique, names like Derek Lam and Comme des Garçons are alongside an in-house collection of coats, shoes and handbags.

Noodle Stories (**D** D4)
→ *8323 W 3rd St (Sweetzer) Tel. (323) 651-1782; Mon-Sat 10am–6pm; Sun noon–5pm*
Find high-concept designers like Junya Watanabe, Sofie D'Hoore and Martin Margiela.

John Varvatos (**D** C4)
→ *8800 Melrose Ave (Robertson); Tel. (310) 859-2791; Mon-Sat 11am–7pm; Sun noon–5pm*
This designer menswear shop sits at the nexus of two shopping arteries: trendy Robertson and haute Melrose.

Book Soup (**D** C3)
→ *8818 W Sunset Blvd (Larrabee); Tel (310) 659-3110; Daily 9am–10pm*
In business for more than 30 years, this fantastic atmospheric independent bookshop has more than 60,000 titles in stock.

Melrose Place (**D** D3)
This groomed, tree-lined street has small shops covered in bougainvillea or ivy, courtyards with boxwood and fountains: **Me & Ro** (no. 8405); **Santa Monica Novella** (no. 8411); **Carolina Herrera** (no. 8441); **Oscar de la Renta** (no. 8446); **Chloe** (no. 8448); **Frédéric Fekkai** (no. 8457).

Melrose Avenue (**D** C-E4)
→ *Almond to Edinburgh*
Maxfield (no. 8825); **Soolip Paperie and Press** (no. 8646); **Marc by Marc** (no. 8410); **Diane von Furstenberg** (no. 8407); **Marc Jacobs Collection** (no. 8400); **Decades** (no. 8214); **Fred Segal** (no. 8100); **Betsey Johnson** (no. 8050); **Miu Miu** (no. 8025).

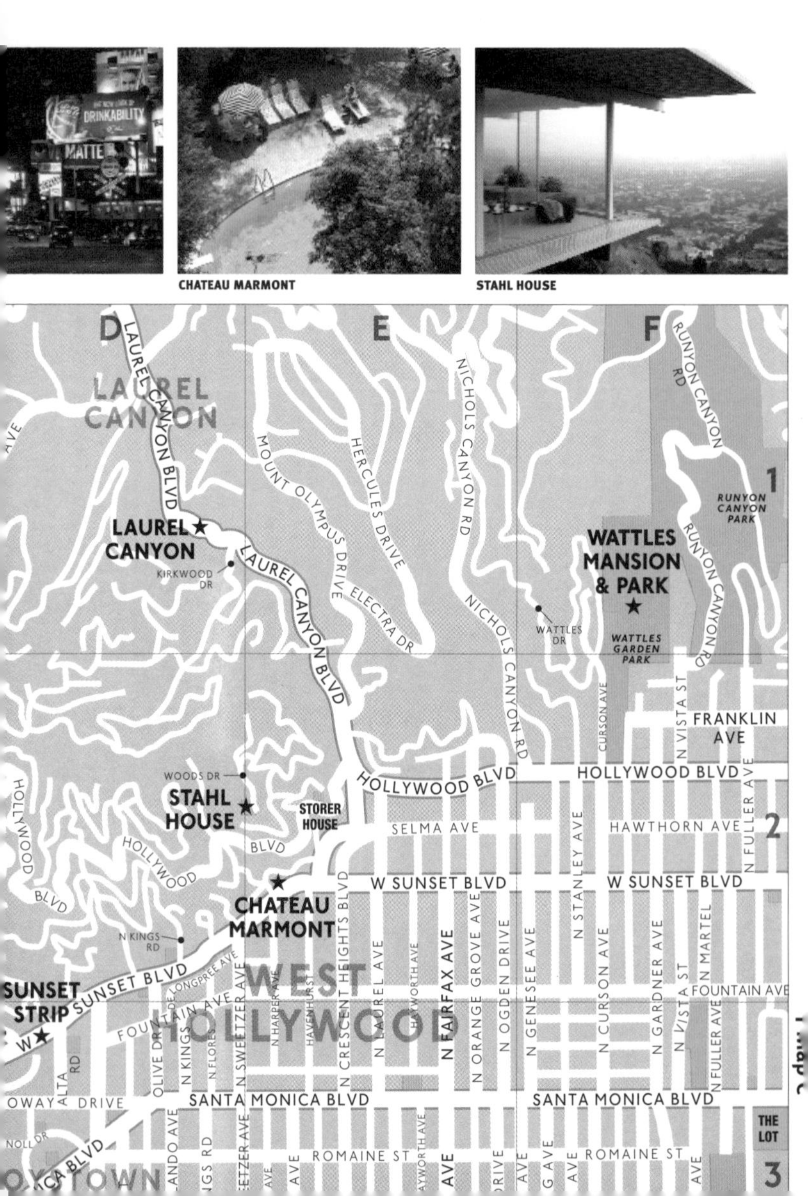
CHATEAU MARMONT
STAHL HOUSE
LAUREL CANYON
LAUREL CANYON BLVD
MOUNT OLYMPUS DRIVE
HERCULES DRIVE
ELECTRA DR
NICHOLS CANYON RD
RUNYON CANYON RD
RUNYON CANYON PARK
WATTLES MANSION & PARK
WATTLES DR
WATTLES GARDEN PARK
KIRKWOOD DR
WOODS DR
STORER HOUSE
HOLLYWOOD BLVD
FRANKLIN AVE
SELMA AVE
HAWTHORN AVE
W SUNSET BLVD
SUNSET STRIP
SUNSET BLVD
N KINGS RD
WEST HOLLYWOOD
FOUNTAIN AVE
SANTA MONICA BLVD
ROMAINE ST
N FAIRFAX AVE
N CRESCENT HEIGHTS BLVD
N LAUREL AVE
N ORANGE GROVE AVE
N OGDEN DRIVE
N GENESEE AVE
N STANLEY AVE
N CURSON AVE
CURSON AVE
N GARDNER AVE
N VISTA ST
N MARTEL
N FULLER AVE
N SWEETZER AVE
N HARPER AVE
HAVENHURST
HAYWORTH AVE
N FLORES
OLIVE DR
DE LONGPRE AVE
ALTA RD
THE LOT

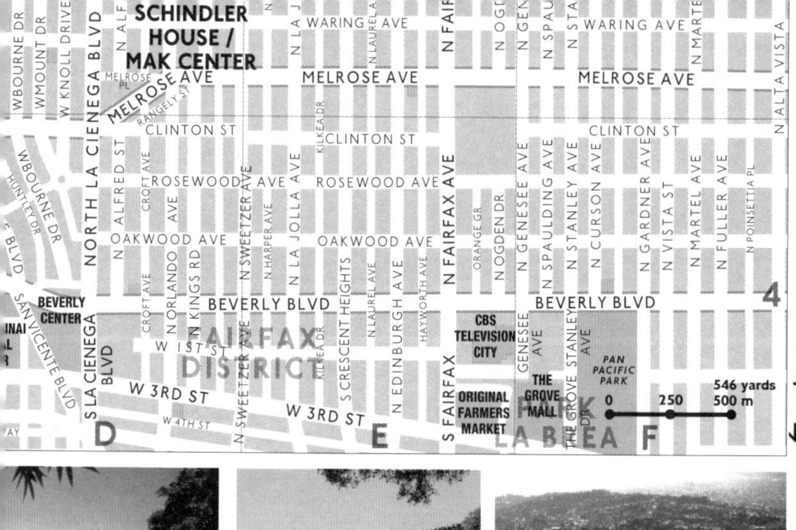

WATTLES MANSION & PARK

LAUREL CANYON

hl family, the home is
ilable for tours (by appt).
Robertson
ulevard (**D** C4)
Beverly Blvd to 3rd St
s shopping district has
reased in notoriety –
nks to overexposed
ebutantes' spending
ees – outdistancing its
fied Rodeo Drive
nterpart in sheer star
ver. Paparazzi swarm
ut, looking for their next
t: Paris Hilton at
tique Kitson or J.Lo
oling salad on the Ivy's
ic patio.
'acific Design
ter (**D** C4)
'687 Melrose Ave (San Vicente); Tel. (310) 657-0800 Mon-Fri 9am–5pm
The 14-acre campus comprises three gargantuan buildings in blue, green or red glass cladding, each designed by Cesar Pelli in three different decades. The PDC houses 130 furniture and design showrooms; Wolfgang Puck has two restaurants; Elton John gives his annual Oscar party and AIDS fund-raiser here.

★ Schindler House/ MAK Center (**D** D3)
→ 835 N Kings Rd (Willoughby); Tel. (323) 651-1510; Wed-Sun 11am–6pm
R. M. Schindler first encountered Los Angeles when Frank Lloyd Wright appointed him to oversee the building of Hollyhock House. Schindler then established his legacy with the design of his own residence; the cooperative live/work space intended for two couples challenged the notions of a conventional home. Converted into a museum in 1994, the MAK Center continues the work of promoting avant-gardist thought through architecture.

★ Wattles Mansion & Park (**D** F1)
→ 1824 Curson Ave (Hollywood)
Tel. (323) 644-6252
Designed in 1907 by local architects Myron Hunt and Elmer Grey for Nebraska banker Gordon Wattles as a winter home. The 50-acre park, open to the public, has four themed gardens, including a Japanese one with teahouse.

★ Laurel Canyon (**D** D1)
This funky street – which looks much as it did in the late 1960s, when music giants Leonard Cohen, Frank Zappa, Stephen Stills, the Mamas and the Papas, Carole King, and Joe Cocker lived there – winds up over the hills from Sunset to the San Fernando Valley and is worth a drive.

RODEO DRIVE

ACADEMY OF MOTION PICTURE ARTS AND SCIENCES

★ **Hammer Museum** (off **E** A1)
→ *10899 Wilshire Blvd (Westwood); Tel. (310) 443-7000; Tue-Sun 11am–7pm (9pm Thu; 5pm Sun)*
Created in 1990 to exhibit the collections of Armand Hammer, including the largest number outside France of works by French caricaturist and painter Honoré Daumier, the museum has since evolved into the city's most dynamic institution for the arts. Programming features established and emerging figures from art, literature, pop culture, even indie rock. The 295-seat Billy Wilder Theater is home to UCLA's Film & TV Archive and Cinematheque.

★ **The Paley Center for Media** (**E** B1)
→ *465 Beverly Dr. (Santa Monica); Tel. (310) 786-1091 Wed-Sun noon–5pm*
This West Coast branch opened in 1996 at a Richard Meier-designed location. Patrons can access nearly 150,000 TV episodes, commercials or radio programs from the extensive media library or enjoy the day's screening in the 150-seat theater. The annual PaleyFest (in April), features talks with television's biggest and most current players.

★ **Rodeo Drive** (**E** B1)
→ *Rodeo Dr. (between Wilshire and Santa Monica)*
It once had a bridle path down the center but it has long been synonymous with the biggest brand names: Chanel, Valentino, Cartier, Tiffany & Co., Dior. While most of the storefronts are surprisingly unassuming, the Rem Koolhaas-designed Prada boutique (no. 343) is a postmodern stunner.

★ **Academy of Motion Picture Arts and Sciences** (**E** C1)
→ *8949 Wilshire Blvd (La Peer); Tel. (310) 247-3000 Tue-Fri 10am–5pm; Sat-Sun noon–6pm*
This is the home of the Oscars. Aside from housi the daily operations of th 6,000-member professio organization, the buildin has two galleries dedicat to special exhibits coveri topics from Fellini and period costumes to anim and Akira Kurosawa. There's also a 1,012-seat theater for screenings.

★ **Museum of Tolerance** (**E** B3)
→ *9786 Pico Blvd (Roxbury Tel. (310) 553-8403 Daily 10am (11am Sun)–5p*
Established in 1993 by th Simon Wiesenthal Cente the museum's most visit

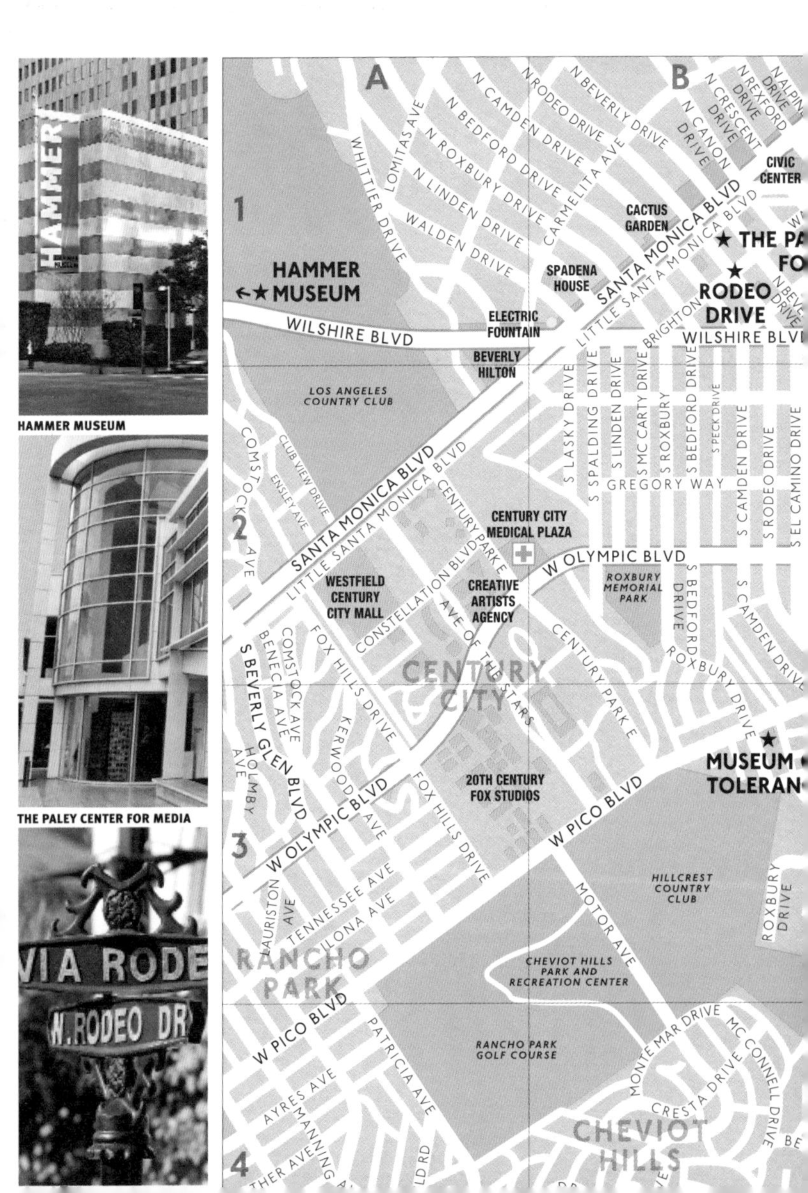

HAMMER MUSEUM

THE PALEY CENTER FOR MEDIA

Beverly Hills fully lives up to its gilded image. The rolling hills and groomed, palm-tree-lined streets of the residential flats hold palatial estates, while downtown sidewalks are bustling with tourists, wheeler-dealers doing lunch, or housewives with big expense accounts. Just south, kosher delis and faith-based centers bear witness to the Jewish stronghold of the South Robertson district. And Culver City is L.A.'s latest Cinderella story. Once an illustrious participant in moviemaking, it has now had a rebirth due to the concentrated emergence of art galleries and successful eateries in the last decade.

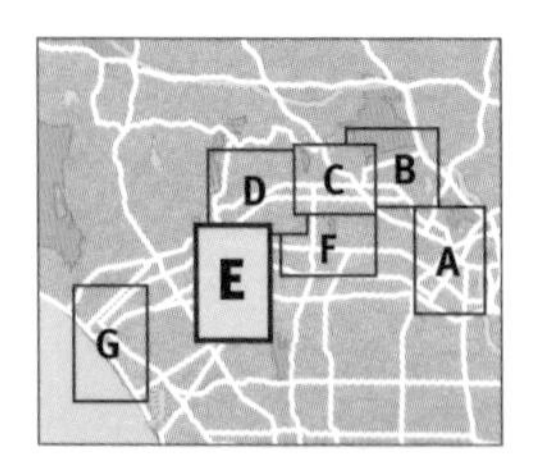

THE BAZAAR (AT SLS HOTEL)

CLEMENTINE

RESTAURANTS

Tender Greens (**E** C5)
→ *9523 Culver Blvd (Cardiff) Tel. (310) 842-8300; Daily 11.30am–9pm (10pm Fri-Sat)*
No omnivore's dilemma here. Locally sourced, sustainable goods create sophisticated salads topped with pole-caught albacore tuna or grilled free-range chicken. Soul-satisfying hot dishes like flatiron steak with mashed potatoes are also menu items. Beer and wine. $10.

Craft/Craftbar (**E** A2)
→ *10100 Constellation Blvd (Century Park E); Tel. (310) 279-4180; Mon-Fri 11.30am–2.30pm, 5.30–10pm; Sat 5.45–10pm; Sun 5–9pm*
Both are from celebrity mastermind Tom Colicchio: Craftbar occupies the front lounge and terrace, serving downsized portions of lamb belly or short rib ravioli; Craft is the formidable steak house, with sumptuous meats, seafood and seasonal produce. $8/ $30.

The Bazaar (at SLS Hotel) (**E** D1)
→ *465 N La Cienega Blvd (Clifton); Tel. (310) 246-5555 Mon-Fri 3–11pm; Sat-Sun 11am–11pm*
Spanish chef and impresario José Andrés presents a multifaceted experience. Two dichotomous dining rooms designed by Philippe Starck host a tapas menu that marries traditional (braised veal cheeks, scallops Romesco) with the freakishly innovative (liquid mozzarella, foams, reductions, shoots and such). More gustatory chicanery at the central bar and the patisserie. Tapas $8–12.

The Wolfgang Puck empire
L.A.'s most famous chef has five local restaurants. **Spago** (*176 N Canon Dr. at Wilshire, Tel. (310) 385-0880,* **E** C1) is his grand signature. If time and money are no objects, indulge in one of the chef's tasting menus ($95–170). Also worth a visit: **Cut** (*9500 Wilshire Blvd at Beverly; Tel. (310) 276-8500,* **E** B1) At the bar or at tables in this sleek, modern wood, chrome and black leather update on a steak house in the Beverly Wilshire Hotel, try the kobe steak sashimi with spicy radishes or the filet mignon carpaccio with white truffles. $24.

Fraiche (**E** C5)
→ *9411 Culver Blvd (Main) Tel. (310) 839-6800; Daily*

RK DOUGLAS THEATRE

THE CHEESE STORE OF BEVERLY HILLS

LE LABO

11.30am–2.30pm, 5.30pm–midnight; closed Sat lunch
This gastronomic gem serves a French-Italian menu of warm mushroom and arugula salad, *boudin noir* on lentils and house-made charcuterie. The jacaranda-sheltered patio is a great spot for al fresco dining and drinks. $22.

Matsuhisa (**E** D2)
→ *129 N La Cienega Blvd (Wilshire); Tel. (310) 659-9639; Mon-Fri 11.45am–2.15pm, 5.45–10.15pm; Sat-Sun 5.45–10.15pm*
This is the birthplace of Nobu. While a flashier outpost resides right up the street, purists abide by this humble, well-worn original for masterful sushi and caviar-inflected fusion inventions. Reserve well in advance and don't be surprised to see Robert De Niro in the house – he and Nobu are business partners. $40.

BAKERIES, DELIS

Sprinkles (**E** B1)
→ *9635 Little Santa Monica Blvd (Bedford); Tel. (310) 274-8765; Mon-Sat 9am–7pm; Sun 10am–6pm*
The sugar-fueled fad had surprising staying power in this (self-billed) world's first cupcake-exclusive bakery. The back wall indicates the day's flavors. There's coffee, tea or milk to wash it all down.

Clementine (**E** A2)
→ *1751 Ensley Ave (Santa Monica); Tel. (310) 552-1080 Mon-Fri 7am–7.30pm; Sat 8am–5pm*
A lovely spot to while away the afternoon over artisanal sandwiches, farm-to-table salads and a refreshingly tall glass of the homemade ginger limeade. Be sure to try a cookie or brownie or the entire assortment of baked goodness.

Nate n' Al (**E** B1)
→ *414 N Beverly Dr. (Brighton); Tel. (310) 274-0101; Daily 7am–9pm*
Located in the heart of downtown Beverly Hills, this deli-to-the-stars serves up celebrity sightings along with its signature matzo brie.

BARS, THEATERS

Mandrake (**E** D4)
→ *2692 S La Cienega Blvd (Venice); Tel. (310) 837-3297 Tue-Sat 5pm–midnight (1am, Fri-Sat); Sun-Mon 6pm–midnight*
The front is practically anonymous aside from the small neon sign simply stating 'BAR.' The space inside, however, is a rustic, wood-paneled haven for artists, gallery owners and high-minded barflies.

Culver City theaters
Culver City's revitalized downtown is bookended by the **Kirk Douglas Theatre** (*9820 Washington Blvd at Hughes, Tel. (213) 628-2772*, **E** C6) which, as a part of L.A.'s premier Center Theatre Group, debuts contemporary plays – and the **Actors' Gang**, a groundbreaking repertory that has taken residence in the historic Ivy Substation (*9070 Venice Blvd at Exposition, Tel. (310) 838-4264*, **E** C5).

SHOPPING

Le Palais Gourmet (**E** B1)
→ *401 N Canon Dr. (Brighton); Tel. (310) 271-7922; Mon-Sat 10am–6pm*
Over 250 exotic and elaborate teas, including a white tea made from rosebuds, fill this beautiful boutique.

The Cheese Store of Beverly Hills (**E** B1)
→ *419 N Beverly Dr. (Brighton); Tel. (310) 278-2855; Mon-Sat 10am–6pm; Sun noon–5pm*
This *fromagerie* is in a league of its own. The inventory boasts the rarest and the stinkiest from all over the world as well as a considerable array of goat's- and sheep's-milk cheeses. Tasting events sell out quickly.

Le Labo (**E** D1)
→ *8385 W 3rd St (Orlando) Tel. (323) 782-0411 Daily 11am–7pm (5pm Sun)*
From Grasse, a perfumery whose fragrances are blended by hand in a stylish mock laboratory setting. Home fragrances and candles are also available.

Department store row (**E** B1)
→ *9570–9700 Wilshire Blvd (Camden to McCarty)*
Get your pocketbooks ready. Neiman Marcus, Saks Fifth Avenue, and Barneys take up three consecutive blocks of Wilshire Boulevard, totaling 600,000 sq. ft of upscale retail space.

Ron Herman (**E** B1)
→ *325 N Beverly Dr. (Dayton) Tel. (310) 550-0910; Mon-Sat 10am–6pm; Sun noon–5pm*
Synonymous with SoCal style, it underscores L.A.'s penchant for T-shirts and jeans at couture prices; also credited with putting Phillip Lim on the map; three additional locations in the city.

↑Map D

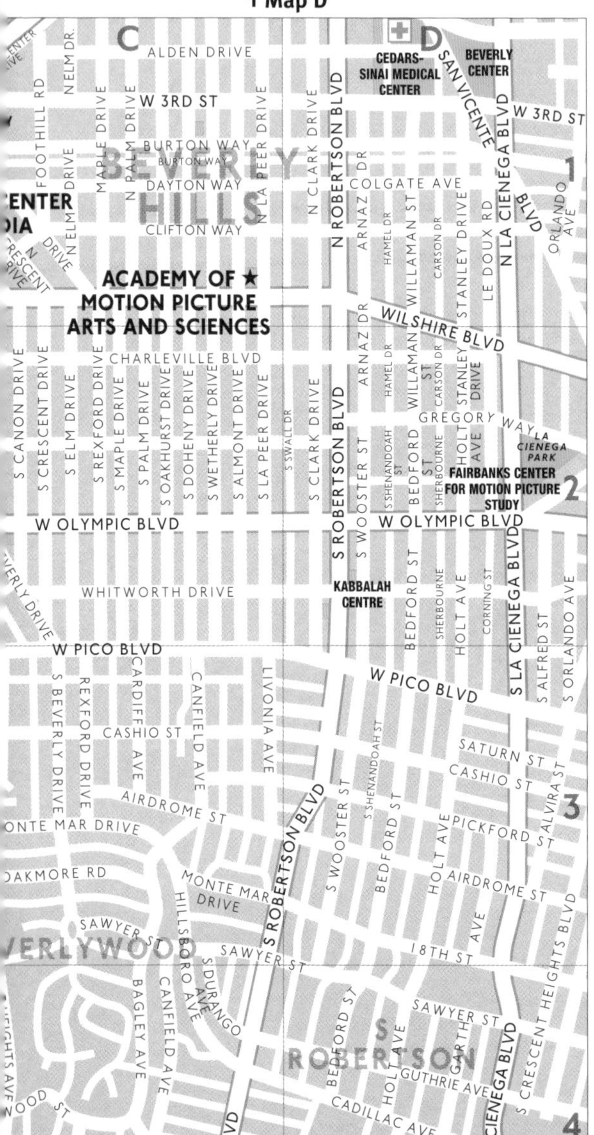

MUSEUM OF TOLERANCE

CULVER HOTEL

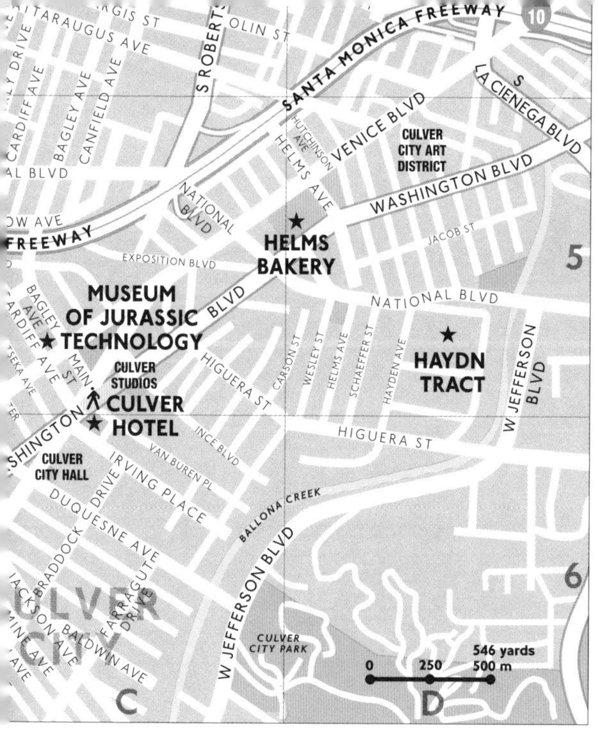

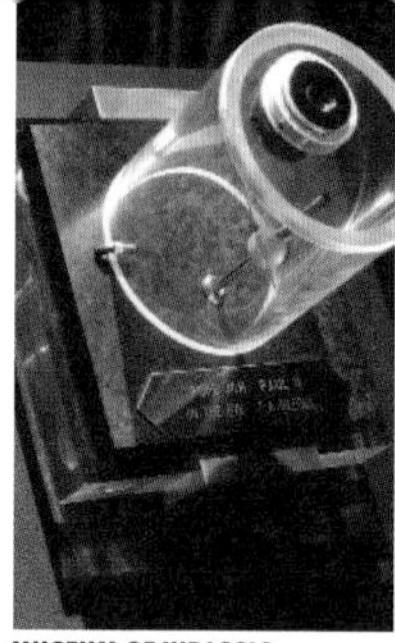

MUSEUM OF JURASSIC TECHNOLOGY

HAYDEN TRACT / THE BEEHIVE

tion focuses on the
ocaust. The Tolerancenter
multimedia installation
mining the issue of
olerance writ large;
sentations include a
onicle of the civil rights
vement and a film
osing human rights
se in Rwanda.

lelms Bakery (**E** C-D5)
758 Venice Blvd
t stores open daily;
v.helmsbakerydistrict.com
s height, Helms Bakery
vered goods directly to
tomers across Southern
fornia, even supplying
ad for the 1932
npics and *Apollo 11*'s
lmark mission to the moon. Today, the grand Art Deco edifice is a commercial/retail center for home furnishings and food. Due east along Washington and La Cienega boulevards is the Art District, featuring L.A.'s most cutting-edge galleries (*www.ccgalleryguide.com*).

★ **Culver Hotel** (**E** C6)
→ *9400 Culver Blvd (Helms)*
Tel. (310) 558-9400
John Wayne was once an owner who, according to legend, had acquired the elegant building from Charlie Chaplin in a poker game. A stone's throw from Culver Studios, the hotel was a part-time residence for many Hollywood stars such as Greta Garbo, Clark Gable, Buster Keaton and Ronald Reagan. Nearly the entire colony of Munchkins lived here during the filming of *The Wizard of Oz*.

★ **Museum of Jurassic Technology** (**E** C5)
→ *9341 Venice Blvd (Main)*
Tel. (310) 836-6131; Thu 2–8pm; Fri-Sun noon–6pm
Such curiosities as the portrait of a 17th-century horned woman, detritus from trailer parks, and the stink ant of Cameroon, are on display. The MJT is less a museum than a work of art critiquing the role of academic institutions and the curating of knowledge. Founder David Wilson is a MacArthur Genius Award Fellow.

★ **Hayden Tract** (**E** C5)
→ *Between Hayden Ave and Jefferson Blvd; National Blvd and Higuera St*
The work of architect Eric Owen Moss has transformed this former industrial district. Postmodern and highly conceptual structures – part of the ongoing Conjunctive Points Development project – include the Beehive, the Umbrella, and such award-winners as Slash & Backslash.

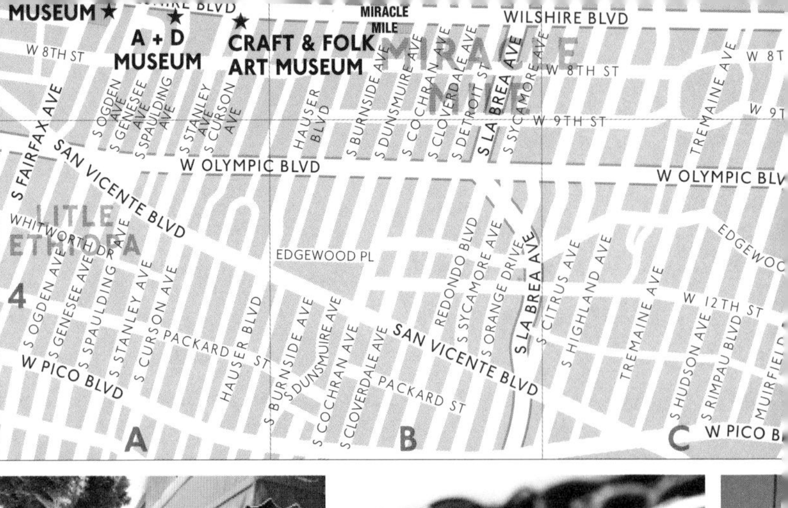

LARCHMONT VILLAGE

LARCHMONT VILLAGE

WILSHIRE

★ **The Original Farmers Market** (**F** A2)
→ *6333 W 3rd St (Fairfax) Mon-Sat 9am–9pm (8pm Sat); Sun 10am–7pm*
In 1934 this market was an empty lot situated on the property of the Gilmore Oil Company that attracted a tailgate gathering of farmers and their wares. It still retains its old-time charm and is always popular for breakfast.

★ **Museum Row** (**F** A3)
Five museum complexes are clustered along a half-mile stretch of Wilshire Boulevard, hence the very apt designation. Hancock Park runs along the north end of the block, a picturesque setting to cool your museum-hopping feet.

★ **Los Angeles County Museum of Art (LACMA)**
→ *no. 5905*
Tel. (323) 857-6000; Mon-Tue, Thu-Fri noon–8pm (9pm Fri); Sat-Sun 11am–8pm
The largest art institution west of the Mississippi, the 20-acre campus grows even bigger. The 2008 opening of the Renzo Piano-designed Broad Contemporary Art Museum (BCAM) – a 60,000 square foot exhibition space displaying among other artists the Koonses and Basquiats of benefactor Eli Broad – and the Grand Entrance – a dazzling piazza bedecked with palm trees and 202 refurbished lampposts – marked the first phase of LACMA's 'Transformations.' The Resnick Pavilion, a freestanding building for special exhibitions, is slated for 2010.

★ **Page Museum / La Brea Tar Pits**
→ *no. 5801; Tel. (323) 934-7243; Daily 9.30am–5pm*
Over 3 million fossils – dating back 40,000 years and representing some 600 species of flora and fauna – have been recovered from the tar pits. Reconstructed skeletons of woolly mammoths and saber-tooth cats are displayed at the adjacen Page Museum. Scientist work are also on view in the fishbowl laboratory.
★ Everyday objects and handicrafts from around the world are on display at the **Craft and Folk Art Museum** (*no. 5800; Tel. (323) 937-4230; Tue-T 11am–5pm; Sat-Sun noon–6pm*); The **Petersen Automotive Museum** (*no. 6060; Tel. (323) 930-2277; Tue-Sun 10am–6pm*) has four floors of exhibi and more than 150 rare classic cars, trucks and motorcycles;

↑ Map C

THE ORIGINAL FARMERS MARKET

LACMA

PETERSEN AUTOMOTIVE MUS

A conversation about Los Angeles would not be complete without addressing Wilshire Boulevard, the major artery that runs nearly 16 miles from downtown to the sea, and which was once promoted as the 'Fifth Avenue of the West.' Today the thoroughfare traverses a diversity of neighborhoods – Koreatown, for example, is adjacent to affluent Windsor Square – and reveals Art Deco treasures. The famous 1/16-portion known as Miracle Mile was thusly named for the commercial and architectural accomplishments that arose in the tar-riddled land between Fairfax and La Brea avenues.

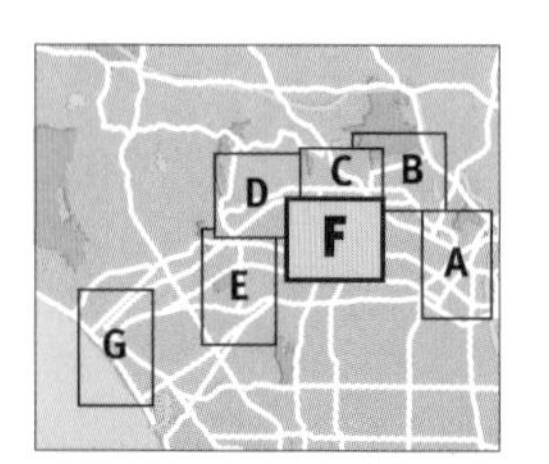

BLD

MILK

RESTAURANTS

Tahoe Galbi (**F** E3)
→ *3986 Wilshire Blvd (Wiltern); Tel. (213) 365-9000 Daily 11.30am–10.30pm*
The all-you-can-eat Korean barbecue special orders up limitless platters of chicken, pork belly and marinated beef for table-side grilling. Buffet $17.

Pizzeria Mozza (**F** C1)
→ *641 N Highland Ave (Melrose); Tel. (323) 297-0101; Daily noon–midnight*

Osteria Mozza (**F** C1)
→ *6602 Melrose Ave (Highland); Tel. (323) 297-0100; Mon-Fri 5.30–11pm, Sat-Sun 5–11pm (10pm Sun)*

Mozza2Go (**F** C1)
→ *6610 Melrose Ave Tel. (323) 297-1130; Tue-Sun noon–11pm (takeout only)*
The partnership between NYC celebrity chef Mario Batali and La Brea Bakery maven Nancy Silverton powers this Italian triptych. The pizzeria brought nationwide attention to L.A.'s pizza-starved food scene. But it's the osteria's mozzarella bar that provides center stage for Silverton's culinary art. Reservations necessary. Pizzeria $15; osteria $25.

BLD (**F** B2)
→ *7450 Beverly Blvd (Gardner); Tel. (323) 930-9744 Daily 8am–10pm (11pm Sat)*
Breakfast features pancakes, frittatas and omelets. A copious list of salads, sandwiches and burgers is available for lunch, while dinner offers meatier plates. $15–25.

Taylor's Steakhouse (**F** F4)
→ *3361 W 8th St (Ardmore) Tel. (213) 382-8449 Mon-Fri 11.30am–9.30pm (10.30pm Fri); Sat-Sun 4–10.30pm (9.30pm Sun)*
This L.A. institution has been serving the house specialty culotte cut, the tenderest portion of the top sirloin, since 1953. The room is dark and filled with red Naugahyde booths. $25.

Susan Feniger's Street (**F** C1)
→ *742 N Highland Ave (Waring); Tel. (323) 203-0500; Mon-Sat noon–midnight (11pm Mon-Wed); Sun 11am–2.30pm (brunch), 5–10pm*
In a brilliant nod to global street food, Feniger has her own restaurant for takeout or eating in the casual interior space or outdoor patio. The exotic menu includes for lunch such dishes as Japanese shizo shrimp or Jerusalem bread salad; for dinner: noodle soup, curries or

REY

AMERICAN RAGS

KIDROBOT

lamb kofta skewer and falafel salad. $12–32.

Animal (**F** A2)
→ *435 N Fairfax (Oakwood) Tel. (323) 782-9225; Daily 6–11pm (2am Fri-Sat)*
Jon Shook and Food Network's Vinny Dotolo's minimal space. The daily-changing menu is mostly about meat and bacon. For dessert try the famous bacon chocolate crunch bar. $24–37.

Campanile (**F** B3)
→ *624 S La Brea Ave (6th) Tel. (323) 938-1447; Mon-Fri 11.30am–2.30pm, 6–10pm (11pm Thu-Fri); Sat-Sun 9.30am–1.30pm, 5.30–11pm*
In a building once owned by Charlie Chaplin, soaring ceilings and a skylight accentuate a Mediterranean atrium. The award- winning menu includes prime rib topped with olive tapenade and Maine scallops with roasted parsnips and chanterelles. La Brea Bakery is next door. $32.

ICE CREAM PARLORS, BARS, MOVIE HOUSES, CLUBS

Milk (**F** B2)
→ *7290 Beverly Blvd (Alta Vista); Tel. (323) 939-6455 Daily 8am–10pm (11pm Fri-Sat)*
This ice cream shop in the former atelier of designer Richard Tyler serves elaborate sundaes and ice cream sandwiches made with wafer-thin macaroons; also hot foods menu, coffee bar and bakery.

Caffe Brass Monkey (off **F** F3)
→ *3440 Wilshire Blvd (Mariposa); Tel. (213) 381-7047; Daily 10am–2am*
Despite the low-grade decor and low-tech sound system, this divey little bar is the city's favorite place for karaoke.

Silent Movie Theatre (**F** A1)
→ *611 N Fairfax Ave (Melrose) Tel. (323) 655-2510; www.silentmovietheatre.com*
Once this 1942 movie house was the only theater in America dedicated to silent cinema. Today it screens avant-garde, cultic titles. Silent movies every Wed.

El Rey (**F** B3)
→ *5515 Wilshire Blvd (Burnside); Tel. (323) 936-6400; www.theelrey.com*
The midsize room of this Art Deco gem with exceptional acoustics makes it an ideal space to catch the lineup of breakout bands and on-the-verge indie artists.

Busby's East (**F** B3)
→ *5364 Wilshire Blvd (La Brea); Tel. (323) 525-2615 Daily 11am (9am Sat)–2am*
The sprawling, bilevel layout includes three bars, two smoking patios, 40 flat-screen TVs all tuned to a sporting event, pool tables, shuffleboard, darts, a dance floor and live music stage. Breakfast is served on weekends.

SHOPPING

Creatures of Comfort (**F** A1)
→ *7971 Melrose Ave (Fairfax) Tel. (323) 655-7855; Mon-Sat 11am–7pm; Sun noon–6pm*
This minimalist boutique edits an uncommon collection of niche labels: Zero Maria Cornejo, VPL, Alexandre Herchcovitch and Isabel Marant.

Flight Club Los Angeles (**F** A2)
→ *503 N Fairfax Ave (Rosewood); Tel. (323) 782-8616 Daily 12.30–7pm (6pm Sun)*
The prices are high, the customer service frosty, but sneaker freaks can't resist genuflecting before the rare Jordans, Dunks and AF1s that line the walls.

American Rag Cie (**F** B2)
→ *150 S La Brea Ave (2nd) Tel. (323) 935-3154; Mon-Sat 10am–9pm; Sun noon–7pm*
Both men's and women's clothing is the latest and trendiest; the vintage stock is also popular. The home furnishings section has a café.

The Way We Wore (**F** B3)
→ *334 S La Brea Ave (3rd) Tel. (323) 937-0878; Mon-Sat 11am–7pm; Sun noon–6pm*
Owner Doris Raymond selects each item in a vast inventory which spans Victorian frocks to shoes and accessories from the 1980s; couture and designer pieces upstairs.

Vintage shops on Melrose Avenue
→ *Fairfax to La Brea*
A desirable destination for vintage and consignment finds: **Wasteland** (*7428 Melrose Ave at Vista,* **F** B1), **SLOW** (*7474 Melrose Ave at Gardener,* **F** B1), **Crossroads Trading Company** (*7409 Melrose Ave at Martel; Tel. (323) 782-8152,* **F** B1); **Melrose Trading Post**, a flea market (*Sun 9am–5pm*) held at the corner of Fairfax and Melrose (**F** A1).

Kidrobot (**F** A1)
→ *7972 Melrose Ave (Fairfax) Tel. (323) 782-1411; Daily 11am–7pm (6pm Sun)*
The ultra-hip toy company carries boundary-pushing collectibles by the likes of Tokidoki and Frank Kozik.

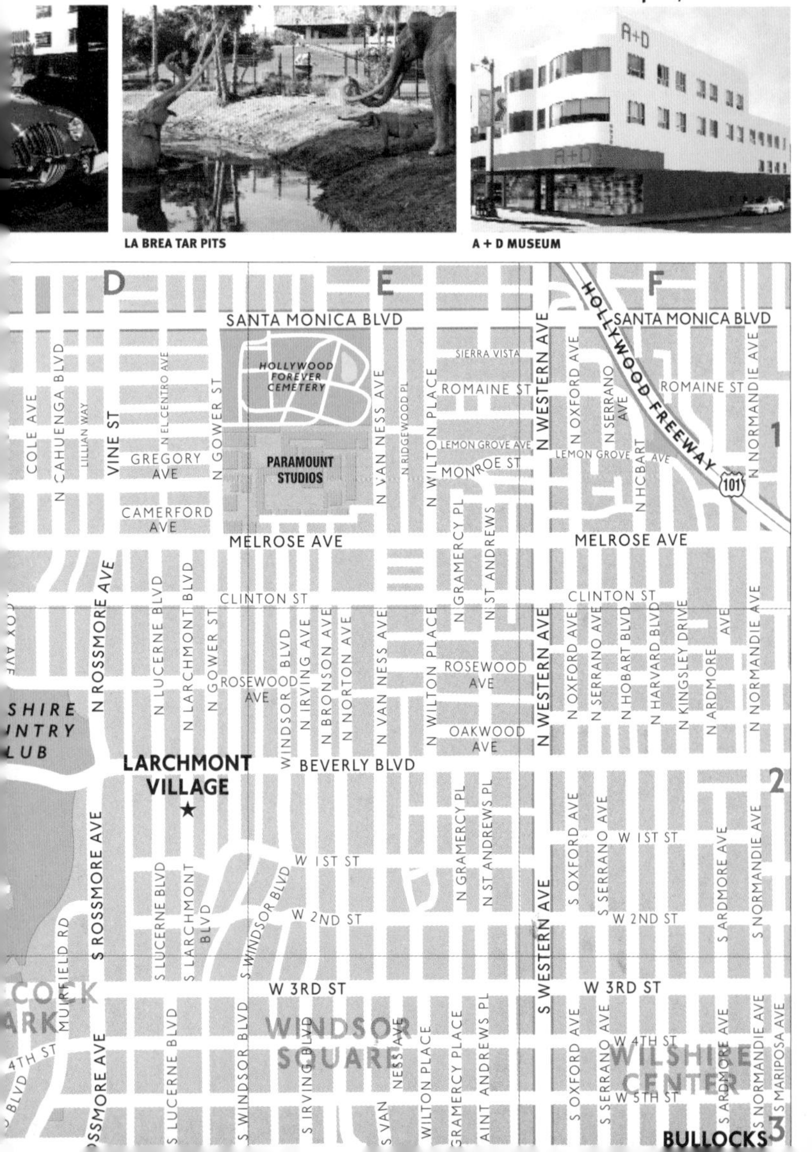

LA BREA TAR PITS

A + D MUSEUM

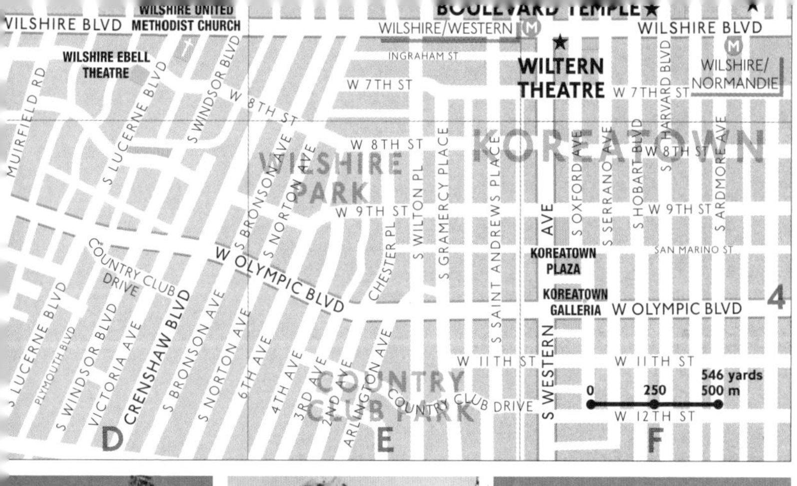

TEMPLE

WILTERN THEATRE

BULLOCKS WILSHIRE

D Museum (*no. 6032; (323) 932-9393; Call for ening times*) is a new seum designed by hard Meier and nsler, with exhibits and formances related to hitecture, design and otography.

Larchmont lage (**F** D2)
Larchmont Blvd (between erly and 3rd)
a slice of small-town rm in the middle of the tropolis, despite roaching corporatization. stretch of sidewalk és, independent efronts and specialty ps serves as an informal Main Street for two of L.A.'s oldest and most affluent neighborhoods, Windsor Square and Hancock Park.

★ **Wilshire Boulevard Temple** (**F** F3)
→ *3663 Wilshire Blvd (Hobart) Tel. (213) 388-2401; Tours by appt; services Fri 6pm, Sat 10.30am; www.wbtla.org*
Of the many churches and cathedrals that line the Wilshire corridor, this monumental Byzantine structure, L.A.'s oldest synagogue, is the only venue listed on the National Register of Historic Places. Completed in 1929, the interior is equally stunning, inlaid with black marble and gold and featuring seven-foot tall murals commissioned by Warner Bros. studio founders Jack, Harry and Albert Warner.

★ **Wiltern Theatre** (**F** F3)
→ *3780 Wilshire Blvd (Western); Tel. (213) 388-1400*
Built in 1931, this theater and the attached Pellissier tower are Art Deco standouts of opulent green terra-cotta, saved from demolition by a ragtag band of preservationists. Meticulous renovations resurrected the site into a premier concert venue, where the most sought-after headliners perform.

★ **Bullocks Wilshire** (off **F** F3)
→ *3050 Wilshire Blvd (Vermont); Tel. (213) 738-6700*
This former store, which opened in 1929, anchors the east end of Wilshire Boulevard's Art Deco landscape. Green-patinated copper accents the distinctive façade and 241-foot tower. After its closing in 1993, the Southwestern Law School acquired and renovated it, and has maintained preservation efforts through the Friends of Bullocks Wilshire. 'Tea and Tour' is opened every summer to the public.

THIRD STREET PROMENADE

WEDNESDAY FARMERS MARKET

★ **Getty Center** (off **G** C1)
→ *1200 Getty Center Dr.*
Tel. (310) 440-7300; Tue-Sun 10am–5.30pm (9pm Sat)
America's wealthiest private arts institution, the J. Paul Getty Trust moved headquarters to this 24-acre, $1.3 billion hilltop campus in 1997, leaving its antiquities collection at the Malibu villa location. The museum houses pre-20th-century European works, including Van Gogh's *Irises*, but the real draw is the Richard Meier-designed complex itself. Italian travertine buildings, manicured gardens and stunning vistas form one of L.A.'s favorite weekend spots.

★ **Gehry House** (**G** B1)
→ *1002 22nd St (Washington)*
Closed to the public
The private residence of famed L.A. architect Frank Gehry. In 1978, the burgeoning architect took a pink bungalow, a 'dumb little house with charm,' and used it as a foundation upon which he expressed his early Deconstructivist style. While a 1993 renovation subdued some subversive design elements, the domicile is still praised as a Gehry exemplar.

★ **Bergamot Station** (**G** D2)
→ *2525 Michigan Ave*
Tel. (310) 829-9125
Most galleries open Tue-Sat 11am–6pm
This art gallery complex, the largest in Southern California, takes its name from the trolley station which operated on the site from 1875 to 1953. Over 30 contemporary art galleries occupy industrial-like warehouses. The Santa Monica Museum of Art relocated here in 1998, bringing its unconventional, non-collecting approach to art curation. The café is a favorite lunch spot for local professionals.

★ **Third Street Promenade** (**G** A-B3)
→ *Between Wilshire and Broadway*
The three-block length of 3rd Street is permanently closed off to traffic, maki this Santa Monica's cent retail district: MAC, Diese Skechers, Banana Repub Starbucks, Sephora, thre stories' worth of Gap are here; street performers a day and well into the nig

★ **Wednesday Farmer Market** (**G** A3)
→ *Arizona Ave (2nd)*
Wed 8.30am–1.30pm
Nearly 100 markets are h

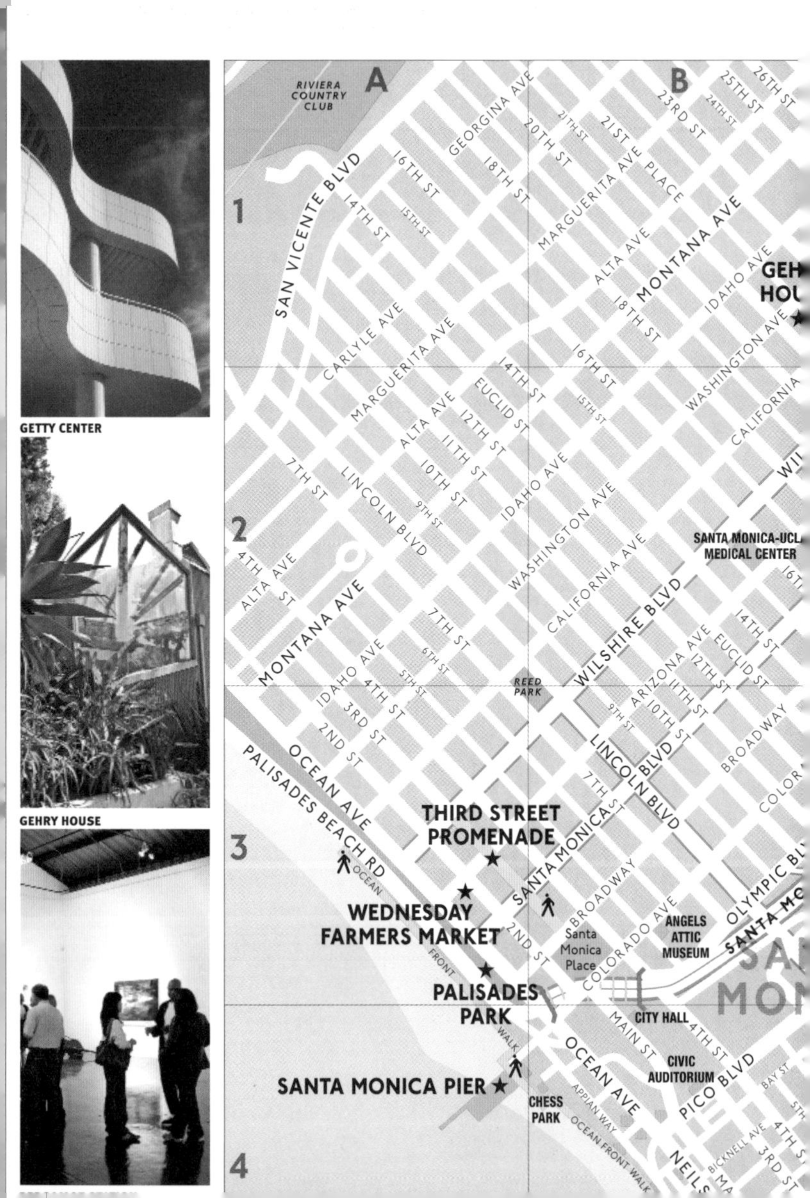
GETTY CENTER
GEHRY HOUSE
RIVIERA COUNTRY CLUB
A
B
1
2
3
4
SAN VICENTE BLVD
GEORGINA AVE
MONTANA AVE
MARGUERITA AVE
CARLYLE AVE
ALTA AVE
IDAHO AVE
WASHINGTON AVE
CALIFORNIA AVE
WILSHIRE BLVD
LINCOLN BLVD
OCEAN AVE
PALISADES BEACH RD
ARIZONA AVE
EUCLID ST
SANTA MONICA-UCLA MEDICAL CENTER
REED PARK
THIRD STREET PROMENADE
WEDNESDAY FARMERS MARKET
PALISADES PARK
SANTA MONICA PIER
CHESS PARK
Santa Monica Place
ANGELS ATTIC MUSEUM
CITY HALL
CIVIC AUDITORIUM
PICO BLVD
OLYMPIC BLVD
BROADWAY
COLORADO AVE
MAIN ST
APPIAN WAY
OCEAN FRONT WALK
BICKNELL AVE
BAY ST

Santa Monica's sandstone bluffs tower above the Pacific Coast Highway, the wide sun-bathed beaches and the pier, site of the 1909 carousel and Pacific Park; farther down the highway, on the way to Malibu, is Will Rogers State Beach, the location for *Baywatch*. Early 20th-century developers built pleasure parks atop piers, while a tobacco magnate audaciously re-created the waterways of Venice. The area fell into disrepair by the 1970s. Remnants of the seaside slums are still visible, notably the Oakwood neighborhood in Venice's eastern sector, as new development plans have revitalized tourism and the housing market once again.

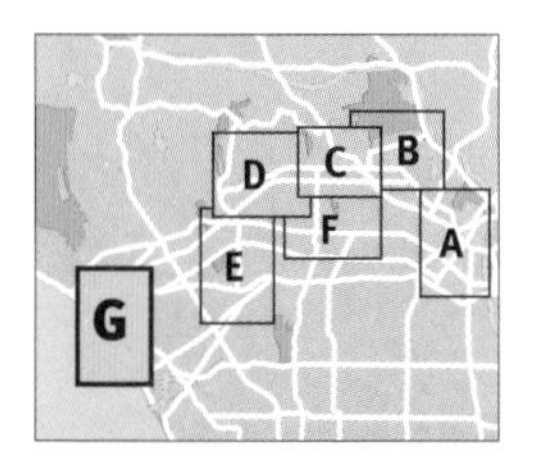

BORDER GRILL

FATHER'S OFFICE

RESTAURANTS

Huckleberry Cafe (**G** B2)
→ *1014 Wilshire Blvd (10th) Tel. (310) 451-2311; Tue-Sun 8am–7pm (5pm Sat-Sun)*
Rustic Canyon Wine Bar & Seasonal Kitchen (**G** B2)
→ *1119 Wilshire Blvd (11th) Tel. (310) 393-7050 Daily 5.30–10.30pm (11.30pm Fri-Sat)*
Two of Santa Monica's most popular eateries. Huckleberry is a daytime hub for artisan pastries, vibrant salads and rotisserie Jidori chicken; candlelit Rustic Canyon offers Mediterranean-inspired dinners; only farmers market ingredients. $11/$24.

Border Grill (**G** B3)
→ *1445 4th St (Broadway) Tel. (310) 451-1655; Daily noon–10pm (11pm Fri-Sat)*
In a raucous, brightly painted room, the 'Two Hot Tamales' Mary Sue Milliken and Susan Feniger have cornered the market in elevating traditional Mexican fare. Artisanal margaritas. $20.

Axe (**G** C5)
→ *1009 Abbot Kinney Blvd (Broadway); Tel. (310) 664-9787; Wed-Sat 11.30am–3pm, 6–10pm (10.30pm Fri-Sat); Sun 5.30–9.30pm; brunch Sat-Sun 9am–3pm*
In this serene, modern space, chef-owner Joanne Moore cooks a simple, organic, seasonal menu – lunch and dinner of little dishes and sides could include a shrimp squid scallion pancake or a main of chicken, lamb chop, fish or beef. $24.

Giorgio Baldi (off **G** A1)
→ *114 W Channel Rd (off Pacific Coast Hwy); Tel. (310) 573-1660); Tue-Sun 6–10pm*
By Santa Monica Canyon, chef-owner Baldi serves up Mediterranean food: fresh fish simply cooked in lemon juice and olive oil or homemade ravioli with ricotta and spinach, risotto with porcini mushrooms. A favorite with surfers, the well-heeled local crowd and celebrities. $30.

Joe's Restaurant (**G** C5)
→ *1023 Abbot Kinney Blvd (Broadway); Tel. (310) 399-5811; Daily noon–2.30pm, 6–10pm (11pm Fri-Sat)*
Chef Joseph Miller prepares quintessential California cuisine of grilled ahi with foie gras or sirloin in balsamic vinaigrette. The three-course lunch prix fixe ($18) is a genuine gourmet deal. $28.

Michael's (**G** A3)
→ *1147 3rd St (Wilshire)*

PATISSERIE

HORIZONS WEST SURF SHOP

ABBOT KINNEY BOULEVARD / COLCHA

Tel. (310) 451-0843; Mon-Fri noon–2.30pm, 6–10pm; Sat-Sun 6–10pm
Michael McCarty opened this popular hangout serving California fare in 1979. He is often there to greet the celebrity clientele who come for the fish burgers, cobb or niçoise salad lunch fare and dinner of classic fish, chicken and steak with Caesar salad. Reservations necessary. $33.

Melisse (**G** B2)
→ *1104 Wilshire Blvd (11th) Tel. (310) 395-0881; Tue-Sat 6–9.30pm (10pm Fri-Sat)*
Michelin gave chef and avid surfer Josiah Citrin two stars for his California take on haute French. Classics are dressed in the bounty of local farms: lobster and passion fruit, duck confit with figs and beets, sweet corn ravioli in truffle sauce. $45.

BAKERIES, CAFÉS, BARS, CLUBS

Jin Patisserie (**G** D5)
→ *1202 Abbot Kinney Blvd (San Juan); Tel. (310) 399-8801; Tue-Sat 10.30am–7pm*
This pastry boutique features couture-worthy confections: architectural cakes of lavender, chocolates infused with pink peppercorn or caramel clove. The attached tea garden is a Zen sanctuary from the hubbub of Abbot Kinney.

Intelligentsia Venice Coffeebar (**G** D5)
→ *1331 Abbot Kinney Blvd (Santa Clara); Tel. (310) 399-1233; Sun-Fri 6am–10pm (11pm Fri); Sat 7am–11pm*
The second West Coast location from the award-winning microroaster. The sleek interior consists of four communal stations, each with a dedicated barista.

Father's Office (**G** A2)
→ *1018 Montana Ave (10th) Tel. (310) 393-2337; Mon-Thu 5pm–1am; Fri 4pm–2am; Sat-Sun noon–midnight (2am Sun); kitchen closes earlier; also in Culver City*
This beer bar, with a rotating selection of 36 crafted brews on tap, is famous for its burger of dry-aged beef.

Air Conditioned Lounge (**G** D2)
→ *2819 Pico Blvd (28th) Tel. (310) 829-3700 Wed-Sat 6pm–2am*

Air Conditioned Supper Club (**G** D5)
→ *625 Lincoln Blvd (Vernon) Tel. (310) 230-5343 Tue-Sun 8pm (7pm Fri)–2am*
Two hotspots in two unlikely Westside locations. The Lounge is an intimate wine bar appointed in moody amber glass; the Supper Club provides a dance floor to go with a nightly schedule of live music.

Harvelle's (**G** B3)
→ *1432 4th St (Santa Monica); Tel. (310) 395-1676 Daily 8pm–2am*
Founded in 1931, it delivers live jazz, R&B, blues and soul in a dark, sexy room where the martini menu is named after the seven deadly sins. Sunday night's long-running Toledo Show features a cabaret of femmes fatales.

Zanzibar (**G** B3)
→ *1301 5th St (Arizona) Tel. (310) 451-2221 Tue-Sun 9pm–2am*
A popular dance lounge with a decor of low-slung couches, Moroccan lamps and curtains. Big DJ names have weekly residences here, and live performances feature from salsa and Afro beat to dance hall and hip-hop.

SHOPPING

Montana Ave (**G** A2-C1)
→ *10th to 17th sts*
Day spas, yoga studios, shops, as well as denim shopping: **Lucky Brand** (*1426 Montana Ave at 15th, Tel. (310) 260-9524*), the blues **Jean Bar** (*1409 Montana Ave at 14th, Tel. (310) 656-7898*), and **Planet Blue** (*800 14th St at Montana, (310) 394-0135*).

Hennessey + Ingalls Art and Architecture Bookstore (**G** A3)
→ *214 Wilshire Blvd (2nd) Tel. (310) 458-9074 Daily 10am–8pm*
Dedicated to all disciplines within the visual arts, this company specializes in rare and out-of-print texts, and also publishes a handful of titles under its own print press.

Horizons West Surf Shop (**G** B4)
→ *2011 Main St (Bicknell) Tel. (310) 392-1122 Daily noon–6pm*
This former site of the legendary Zephyr shop has been landmarked for its role in birthing modern-day surf and skateboarding culture.

Abbot Kinney Blvd
→ *Westminster to Venice*
Bohemia and chic meet on this great street, a few minutes from the beach. Furniture – **Colcha** (no. 1356), **Dewey** (no. 1108), **Digs** (no. 1118); clothing – **Ananda** (no. 1356), **Claudia Milan** (no. 1350), **ecookie** (no. 1639), **Principessa** (no. 1323).

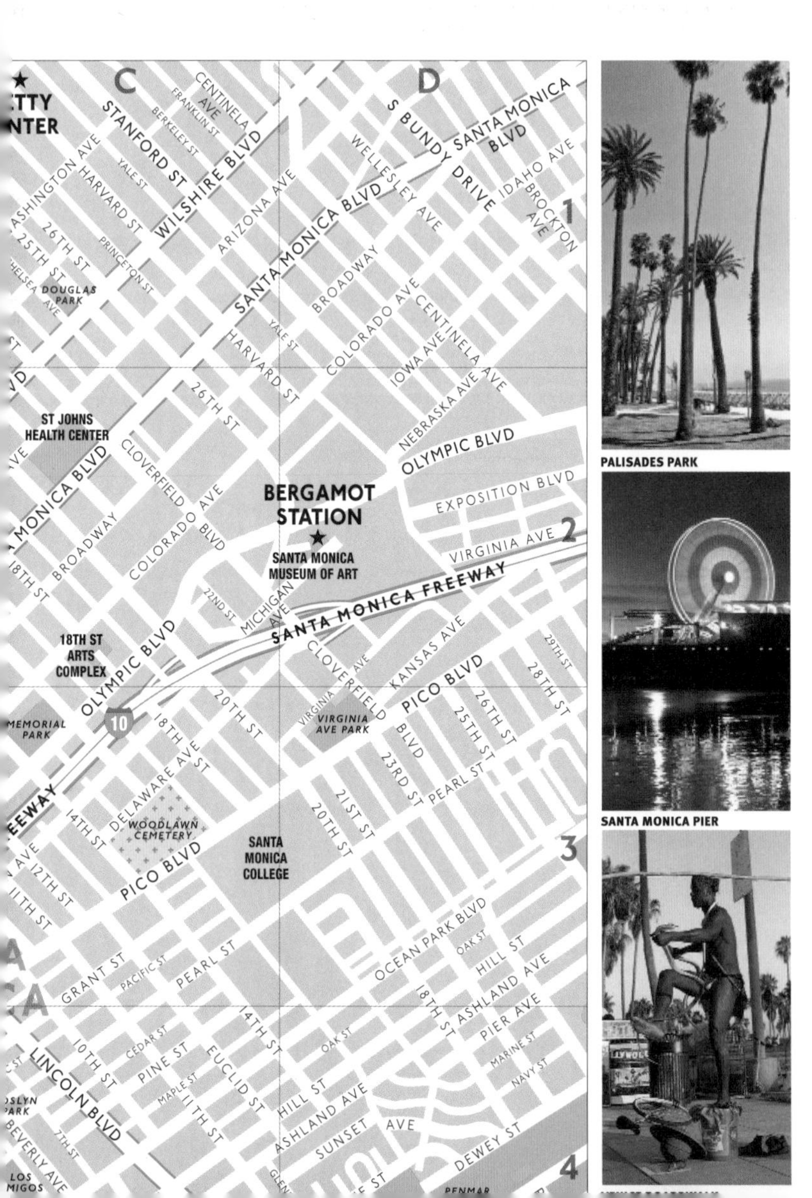

PALISADES PARK

SANTA MONICA PIER

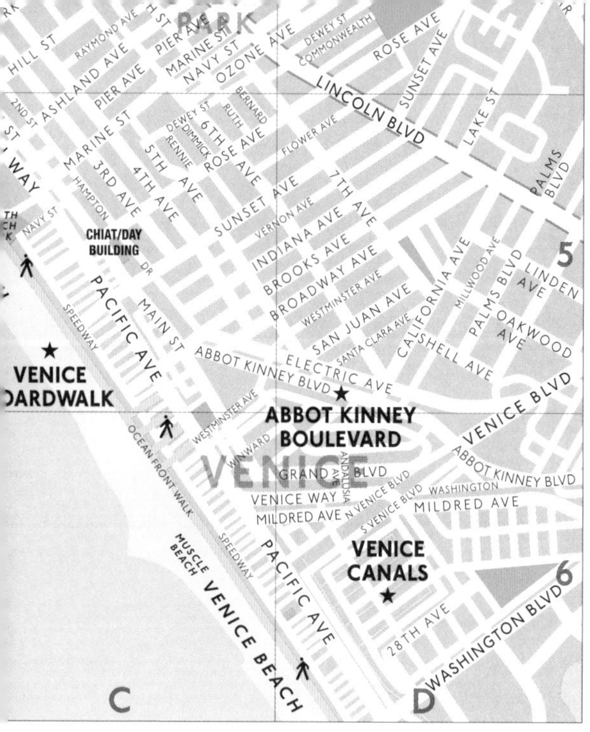

ABBOT KINNEY BOULEVARD

VENICE CANALS

oss L.A. County every ɛk – the Wednesday ɿering is the one for dies. A veritable who's ɔ of chef celebrities also ally shop here. The ection of produce, ɔs and flowers is always k-of-the-season. ed goods and prepared ds are also available.

alisades Park (G A3)
cean Ave (north of San nte to Colorado)
se 26 acres run along bluffs overlooking ta Monica Bay, viding 1.6 miles of athtaking views for the tinual stream of ers, dog walkers, and young families with their prams. The trail gets steeper and more scenic as you head north, away from the tourist-laden pier. During the holidays, large-scale dioramas depicting the Nativity appear in the park.

★ Santa Monica Pier (G A4)
→ *200 Santa Monica Pier*
From the famous arched entryway to the brilliant sunset vistas over the Pacific Ocean, the pier is central to L.A.'s iconic image of sun, surf and sand. Diversions abound, including a trapeze school, a vintage carousel from 1922, and an amusement park complete with roller coaster and the world's only solar-powered Ferris wheel. The pier celebrated its centennial in 2009.

★ Venice Boardwalk (G C5-D6)
A riotous carnival of souvenir vendors, jugglers, sand sculptors, fortune-tellers and fire-breathing performers. Bodybuilders flex their brawn at the world-famous Muscle Beach. The Art Walls offer a public venue for spectacular graffiti-style compositions.

★ Abbot Kinney Boulevard (G C-D6)
→ *Between Brooks and Venice*
Vintage furniture stores, sidewalk cafés, and artists' studios function as an unofficial downtown for the beach city. The annual street festival draws hundreds of thousands of locals and tourists for a final hurrah to summer.

★ Venice Canals (G D6)
Of the original canals, inspired by those in Italy, only six remain, crossed by their original 1905 wooden bridges. The waterfront homes, quaint canals and paths make for a charming scene. It's a private area, but residents don't seem to mind respectful visitors out for a leisurely stroll.

CIVIC CENTER DISTRICT / CITY HALL

ROBINSON MEMORIAL

HUNTINGTON

★ **Rose Bowl** (**H** A1)
→ *1001 Rose Bowl Dr. Tel. (626) 577-3101; Flea market every second Sun of the month 9am–4.30pm*
The New Year's spectacle of the Tournament of Roses Parade ends here. During the rest of the year, the stadium is a mecca for treasure hunters who comb through the bric-a-brac of one of the world's largest flea markets.

★ **Gamble House** (**H** A2)
→ *4 Westmoreland Pl. (Orange Grove); Tel. (626) 793-3334; Tours Thu-Sun noon–3pm; the 2pm tour can be booked in advance*
This century-old masterpiece of wood and stained glass is the most enduring architectural example of the American Arts and Crafts movement. Charles and Henry Greene, forerunners of the form known as the California bungalow, designed the large-scale house for David and Mary Gamble of the Proctor and Gamble Company, who had moved west to settle into retirement.

★ **Norton Simon Museum** (**H** B2)
→ *411 W Colorado Blvd (Orange Grove); Tel. (626) 449-6840; Daily noon–6pm (9pm Fri); free admission first Fri of each month 6–9pm*
This ardent art collector's private collection of European art and South and Southeast Asian statuary includes one of the largest number of works by Edgar Degas. Recent renovations led by Frank Gehry redesigned the idyllic 2-acre Sculpture Garden.

★ **Colorado Street Bridge** (**H** A2)
→ *Colorado Blvd, between Orange Grove and Arroyo*
The majestic bridge spans 150 feet above the Arroyo Seco canyon, forming the western entryway into Pasadena's historic downtown. The landmark is popularly known as 'Suicide Bridge' and considered haunted.

★ **Tournament House Wrigley Gardens** (**H** A
→ *391 S Orange Grove Bl (Arbor); Tel. (626) 449-41 Feb-Aug: free tours Thu 2–*
Among the opulence of Millionaires Row, this mansion was once own by chewing-gum magna William Wrigley Jr before was donated to the city specifically to serve as headquarters for the Tournament of Roses.

★ **Civic Center District** (**H** B-C2)
→ *Between Raymond / Green / Los Robles / Waln*
As the centerpiece of th

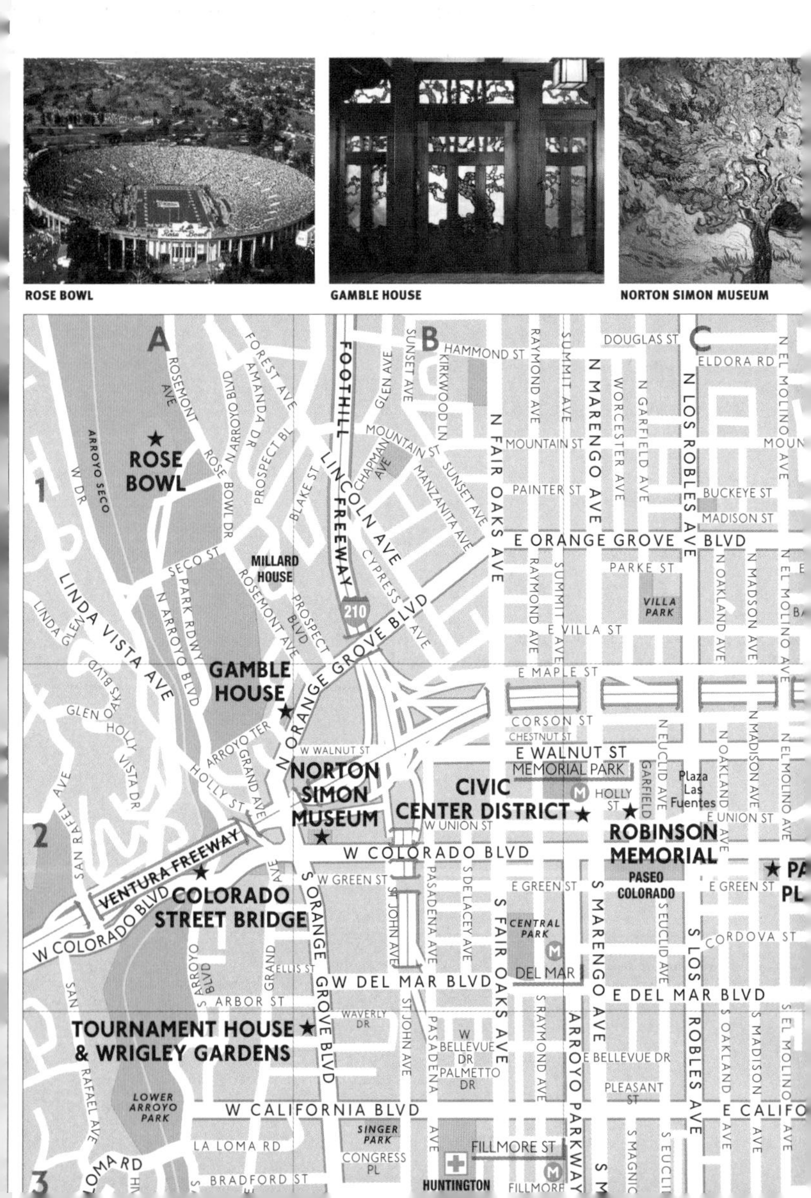

ROSE BOWL

GAMBLE HOUSE

NORTON SIMON MUSEUM

The sunny hamlet of Pasadena is nestled in the San Gabriel Mountains that run along the northern edge of Greater Los Angeles. Steeped in history, the city shows in its architectural topography from the Beaux Arts-bedecked downtown to the American Arts & Crafts apparent in the Craftsman bungalow. Museums have grown from the largesse of retiring tycoons who settled here in the early parts of the 20th century. The area also has, due to the proximity of NASA's Jet Propulsion Laboratory and Cal Tech, a significant community of physicists, rocket scientists and other brainiacs.

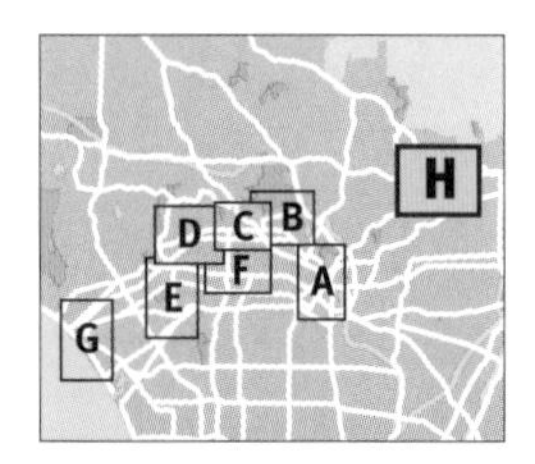

LA GRANDE ORANGE

EURO PANE

RESTAURANTS

The Hat (**H** D1)
→ *491 N Lake Ave (Villa) Tel. (626) 449-1844Daily 9am (10am Sun)–10pm*
The Hat has been dipping its 'world famous' pastrami in au jus since 1951. Other Americana comforts are chili dogs, BBQ beef, burgers, or pastrami burger. Be sure to splurge on an order of fries 'wet' with gravy. $5.

Pie 'n Burger (**H** D3)
→ *913 E California Blvd (Lake); Tel. (626) 795-1123 Mon-Fri 6am–10pm; Sat-Sun 7am–10pm (9pm Sun)*
For some, it has the best pie in the city; for others, the best burger with its housemade Thousand Island dressing. The same Formica counter, swivel stools, even some waitresses have been there since its 1963 inception. $8.

Saladang (**H** B2)
→ *363 S Fair Oaks Ave (Del Mar); Tel. (626) 793-8123 Daily 10am–9.45pm*
Not to be confused with its offshoot, Saladang Song next door, the original is more traditionalist. Favored classics include yellow curry, crab fried rice and pad thai, which is elegantly tucked into an egg crepe; concrete floors and exposed pipes fashion an ultramodern scene. $10.

Elements Kitchen (**H** B2)
→ *107 S Fair Oaks Ave (Green); Tel. (626) 440-0100 Tue-Sun 11am (10am Sat-Sun)–4pm*
A charming lunch and weekend brunch spot. Premium ingredients with a global twist: Madras curry in the chicken salad, truffle oil for the mac n' cheese, and duck confit in the breakfast burrito. $12.

La Grande Orange (**H** B2)
→ *260 S Raymond (Del Mar); Tel. (626) 356-4444 Mon-Fri 11.30am–10pm (11pm Fri); Sat-Sun 11am–11pm (9pm Sun)*
Built into the 1935 Santa Fe Railway Depot, this modern American café recaptures the era with a mahogany bar and a Mission-style patio replete with a fireplace and fountains. The diverse menu includes sashimi appetizers, steaks and taco platters. $19.

Parkway Grill (**H** C3)
→ *510 S Arroyo Pkwy (California) Tel. (626) 795-1001 Mon-Fri 11.30am–2.30pm, 5.30–10pm (11pm Fri); Sat-Sun 5–11pm (10pm Sun)*

LD BUG

LATHER

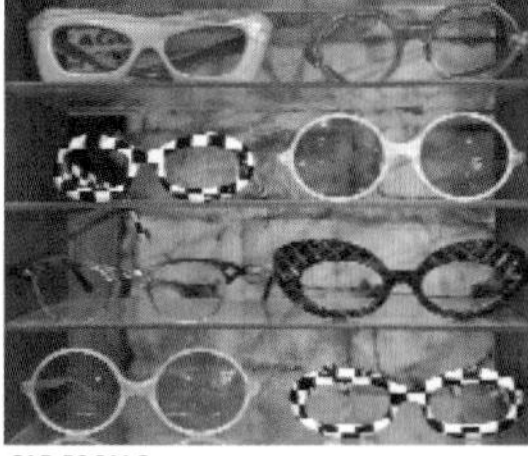
OLD FOCALS

Pasadena's most considered dining destination. An open kitchen and fireplace anchor the spacious room of wooden rafters and brick. A wood-burning oven and grill yield the protein-heavy menu; vegetables and herbs come from the garden out back. $30.

BAKERY, TEAROOM, CAFÉS, BARS

Euro Pane Bakery (**H** D2)
→ *950 E Colorado Blvd, #107 (Mentor)*
Tel. (626) 577-1828; Daily 7am–5.30pm (3pm Sun)
Sumi Chang is a pastry goddess. Droves come daily to buy her chocolate croissants, homemade granola, sizable macaroons accented with hazelnut or sea salt.

Chado Tea Room (**H** B2)
→ *79 N Raymond Ave (Holly)*
Tel. (626) 431-2832
Daily 11.30am–7pm
Stocking over 300 types of specialty teas, the refined, white-linen dining room is great for quick refreshment or a full afternoon service of rich scones and finger sandwiches. Also soups, salads and sandwiches.

Jones Coffee Roasters (**H** B3)
→ *537 S Raymond Ave (California); Tel. (626) 564-9291; Mon-Fri 6.30am–8pm; Sat-Sun 8am–4pm*
The industrial space serves the retail side of the local coffee company. Beans from the family farm in Guatemala are roasted here. Workshops teach brewing or provide introductions to cupping.

Zephyr Coffee House & Art Gallery (**H** F2)
→ *2419 E Colorado Blvd (Sierra Madre)*
Tel. (626) 793-7330; Sun-Tue 8am (9am Sun)–10pm; Wed-Sat 8am–midnight
This 1908 Craftsman cottage is decorated with rotating collections from local artists. There's a hookah in the garden patio and live music several times a month.

Bodega Wine Bar (**H** C2)
→ *260 E Colorado Blvd (Marengo); Tel. (626) 793-4300; Daily 4pm–1am*
Above the Paseo Colorado mall, this stylish bar is unpretentious and welcoming, offering potables by the glass, carafe or entire bottle. Happy hour all night on 'Happy Mondays.'

Old Towne Pub (**H** B2)
→ *66 N Fair Oaks Ave (Holly)*
Tel. (626) 577-6583
Daily 4pm–2am
After 10pm, this divey bar morphs into a live music venue, one of Pasadena's premier stages since 1973, featuring rock, alternative and pop punk acts.

SHOPPING

Vroman's Bookstore (**H** C2)
→ *695 E Colorado Blvd (Oak Knoll); Tel. (626) 449-5320*
Mon-Sat 9am–9pm (10pm Fri-Sat); Sun 10am–9pm
Founded in 1894, this is Southern California's oldest and largest independent bookstore.

Fair Oaks Pharmacy and Soda Fountain (**H** B4)
→ *1526 Mission St (Fair Oaks); Tel. (626) 799-1414*
Mon-Sat 9am–9pm; Sun 10am–7pm
This former rest stop along historic Route 66 still has old-time charm, thanks to a 1990 renovation that restored everything from the stained-glass cabinets to the tiled floors. The vintage soda counter serves the classics: phosphates, rickeys, banana splits. The kitschy gift shop is also amusing.

Distant Lands (**H** B2)
→ *56 S Raymond Ave (Green); Tel. (626) 449-3220*
Mon-Sat 10.30am–8pm (9pm Fri-Sat); Sun 11am–6pm
A global inventory of maps and travel literature, and in the adjoining space apparel, luggage and all sorts of TSA-approved accoutrements.

Lather (**H** B2)
→ *17 E Colorado Blvd (Fair Oaks); Tel. (626) 396-9636*
Mon-Sat 11am–9pm (10pm Fri-Sat); Sun 11am–7pm
The skincare and spa treatment line was founded here. Personalized admixtures can be created at the blending bar.

Gold Bug (**H** B2)
→ *22 E Union St (Fair Oaks)*
Tel. (626) 744-9963
Daily 10am–6pm (5pm Sun)
Everything in this shop tends toward the macabre: mounted rhino beetles, vintage posters of scientific dissections, a colony of glass spider figurines. The jewelry is especially creepy.

Old Focals (**H** B2)
→ *45 W Green St (Fair Oaks)*
Tel. (626) 793-7073; Tue-Sat 11am–7pm; Sun 10am–6pm
The vintage eyewear is affordably priced. The stock is also a boon for Hollywood – 120 pairs were used for the production of *Frost/Nixon*.

COLORADO STREET BRIDGE

TOURNAMENT HOUSE & WRIGLEY GARDENS

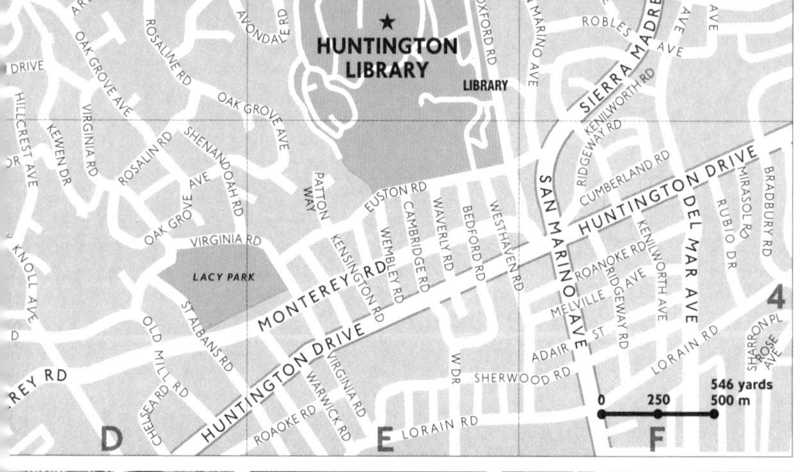

HE GARDENS

PASADENA PLAYHOUSE

L.A. COUNTY ARBORETUM & GARDENS

y Beautiful movement of
1920s, this historic
trict developed around
ee Beaux Arts beauties:
Myron Hunt-designed
blic library to the north,
3,029-seat auditorium,
'ch has hosted, among
er noteworthy events,
Primetime Emmy
ards to the south, and at
heart, the stately, dome-
ped City Hall. The Plaza
Fuentes offers a lovely
oll through fountains and
tile murals.

**Robinson
morial** (**H** C2)
oo N Garfield Ave (Holly)
ated across from City
at the heart of the Civic Center district, these 9-foot sculptures memorialize two of Pasadena's favorite sons: Jackie, whose first game with the Brooklyn Dodgers in 1947 marked the desegregation of Major League Baseball, and his brother, Mack, who won a 200-meter silver medal behind Jesse Owens at the 1936 Berlin Summer Olympics.

★ Pasadena Playhouse (**H** C2)
→ *39 S El Molino Ave (Green)*
Tel. (626) 356-7529
Free backstage tours by appt
Founded in a former burlesque house in 1917, this theatrical group was named the State Theatre of California by the legislature in 1937. Today, it is still one of the nation's premier institutions in developing new works for the American stage.

★ Huntington Library (**H** E3)
→ *1151 Oxford Rd, San Marino*
Tel. (626) 405-2100
Wed-Mon 10.30am–4.30pm (summer hours vary); free admission first Thu of each month with advanced tickets
The library has an archive of 6 million rare books and manuscripts, a highly regarded collection of 18th- and 19th-century British portraiture including Thomas Gainsborough's *Blue Boy* and Thomas Lawrence's *Pinkie*, and 120 acres of themed gardens featuring exotic botanicals from around the world.

★ L.A. County Arboretum & Gardens (off **H** F2)
→ *301 N Baldwin Ave Arcadia; Tel. (626) 821-3222*
Daily 9am–5pm
The 127 acres cultivate a global array of botanicals. Historic buildings also dot the scenic landscape; Queen Anne Cottage was most famously featured in *Fantasy Island*.

LAX TO DOWNTOWN

FlyAway Buses
→ *Every 30 mins (5.30am–12.30am); every hour (1–5am); Non-stop buses to Union Station; $7; wait by the green sign*
Shared-ride vans
→ *24/7; with Prime Time Shuttle or Super Shuttle; $15–20 per person; wait by the orange sign*
Taxi
→ *$40–50, excl. tip. A flat $45 fee to downtown is often negotiable*
Public transportation
→ *24/7; free LAX Shuttle G to Metro Green Line, then two more connections; $1.25; wait by the blue sign*

LAX AIRPORT

THE 101 FREEWAY

THE MISSION-REVIVAL STYLE UNION STATION

Tel. (310) 429-0234; www.veniceonthebeachhotel.com
A two-story bungalow across from Venice Beach with 18 rooms and good amenities – each has a fridge, a microwave, free Wi-Fi and TV. The rooftop deck is a fantastic place to take in the sunset. Attentive service. $130.

Hollywood Hills Hotel (**C** B2)
→ *1999 N Sycamore Ave (Franklin)*
Tel. (323) 874-5089; www.hollywoodhillshotel.com
Less splashy than its sister Magic Castle Hotel at the foot of the hill, this former apartment building offers spacious residence-like accommodations. Ask for a room with a view. $134–164.

Omni Los Angeles at California Plaza (**A** B4)
→ *251 S Olive St (3rd)*
Tel. (213) 617-3300
www.omnihotels.com
Atop Bunker Hill, the recently renovated 17-story, 453-room luxury hotel is practically in MOCA's backyard. Spa, outdoor pool and impeccable service. From $149.

$150–200

Villa Delle Stelle (**C** D3)
→ *6087 Harold Way (Gower)*
Tel. (323) 876-8100
www.villadellestelle.com
In the heart of Hollywood five suites and a detached bungalow, each inspired by a different celebrity. The proprietor is a former wife of Dudley Moore; the 'English Suite' contains personal memorabilia including his disklavier piano. $150–225.

Los Feliz Lodge (**B** D3)
→ *1507 N Hoover St (Sunset)*
Tel. (323) 660-4150
www.losfelizlodge.com
The 'lodge' is four 1920s Spanish courtyard-style cottages and bungalows with private living room, kitchen and bathroom. Quiet, clean, comfortable with eco-conscious furnishings. $150–180.

Maison 140 (**E** B2)
→ *140 Lasky Dr (Charleville)*
Tel. (310) 281-4000; www.maison140beverlyhills.com
Louis XVI chairs and chinoiserie re-create a 5th-arrondissement boudoir in each of the 43 units. It's a boutique hotel in a prime Beverly Hills location: many things – from room to elevator – are petite, and amenities are extra. $155–225.

Garden Cottage B&B (**D** D4)
→ *8318 W 4th St (Sweetzer)*
Tel. (323) 653-5616
http://gardencottagela.com
Two rooms are all there is – a private cottage or a room in the main house – so the setting is quite intimate. Many attractions are within walking distance. $155–185.

Angeleno Hotel
→ *170 N Church Lane (Sunset); Tel. (310) 476-6411*
www.hotelangeleno.com
An upper-level room is highly advisable in this looming 17-story cylinder along the 405 freeway nearby the Getty Center. Outdoor pool, free shuttle (by reservation). Excellent service. $165–180.

Andaz West Hollywood (**D** D2)
→ *8401 Sunset Blvd (Kings)*
Tel. (323) 656-1234
http://westhollywood.hyatt.com
Sunset Strip's 'Riot Hyatt' is now the ultra-sophisticated Andaz, meaning 'personal service' in Hindi. Guests are welcomed with a glass of wine during check-in and the in-room (non-

AIRPORT

Los Angeles International Airport (LAX)
→ *16 miles southwest of downtown; www.lawa.org*
L.A.'s primary airport, it handles nearly all international flights and most domestic ones.
LA/Ontario International Airport
→ *38 miles east; www.lawa.org*
Domestic flights and flights to Mexico.
Long Beach Airport
→ *25 miles south*
Domestic flights.
Bob Hope Burbank Airport
→ *15 miles northwest*
Domestic flights.

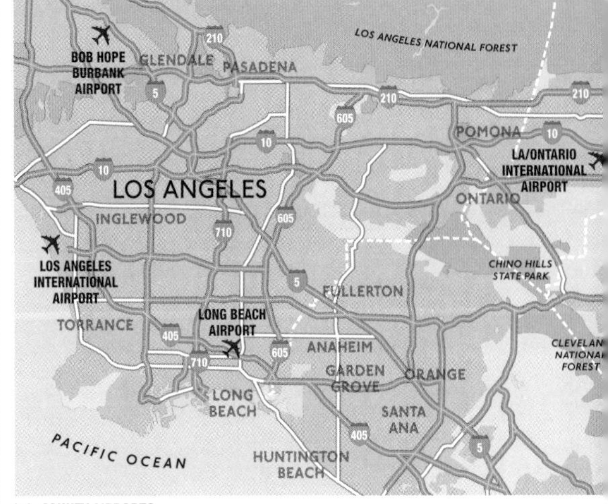

L.A. COUNTY AIRPORTS

- *Prices reflect one double room en suite, based on the lowest rate in high season excluding occupancy tax (14 percent) and breakfast*
- *Parking is usually an expensive additional charge, ranging as high as $25 per day*
- *Booking early and via the Web may reduce prices significantly. Staying in outlying areas is also cheaper*

UNDER $110

Hostelling International Santa Monica (G A3)
→ *1436 2nd St (Santa Monica); Tel. (310) 393-9913 www.hilosangeles.org*
Situated between the hubbub of Third Street Promenade and the beach, the renovated hostel include such facilities as a self-service kitchen, Internet café, laundry and a movie room. Private rooms from $89 (plus $3 per day for nonmembers).
Stay (A B5)
→ *636 S Main St (6th)*
Tel. (213) 213-7829
http://stayhotels.com
This hostel has a vast array of room options – from private queen en suite to bunk beds with shared bath. Free Internet, iPod docking stations, flat screen TVS. From $85 (double en suite).
Millennium Biltmore (A B4)
→ *506 S Grand Ave (5th)*
Tel. (213) 624-1011
www.millenniumhotels.com/millenniumlosangeles
The 1923 Beaux Arts landmark has modestly sized, classically done rooms and a good range of amenities, but don't expect the latest high-tech gadgetry. Note the chandeliers and coffered ceiling in the lobby area. From $109.

$110–150

Farmer's Daughter Hotel (F A2)
→ *115 S Fairfax Ave (Beverly)*
Tel. (323) 937-3930
www.farmersdaughterhotel.com
Its 2003 makeover gave the low-budget motel close to the Farmers Market (see **F**) a glossier, kitschier personality. Dressed in wood paneling and gingham, the themed site has large rooms and a friendly, efficient staff. $119–149.
Hollywood Heights Hotel (C C2)
→ *2005 N Highland Ave (Franklin); Tel. (323) 876-8600; www.hollywoodheightshotel.com*
A former Holiday Inn with modish upgrades, but in prime location: both the Hollywood Bowl to the north and the main drag to the south are within walking distance $119–169.
The Standard Downtown (A B4)
→ *550 S Flower St (6th)*
Tel. (213) 892-8080
www.standardhotels.com/los-angeles
The rooftop pool with cherry red lounging pod is very Hollywood-at-pla Modern, very minimal decor, service uneven, b rates are low. From $12
O Hotel (A B4)
→ *819 S Flower St (8th)*
Tel. (213) 623-9904
www.ohotelgroup.com
Behind the sleek black-on-glass façade t 67 rooms are narrow wi a stylishly minimalist lo the bathrooms, howeve may feel a bit too small for comfort. In-room sp $127–179.
Venice on the Beach (G D6)
→ *2819 Ocean Front Walk (Washington)*

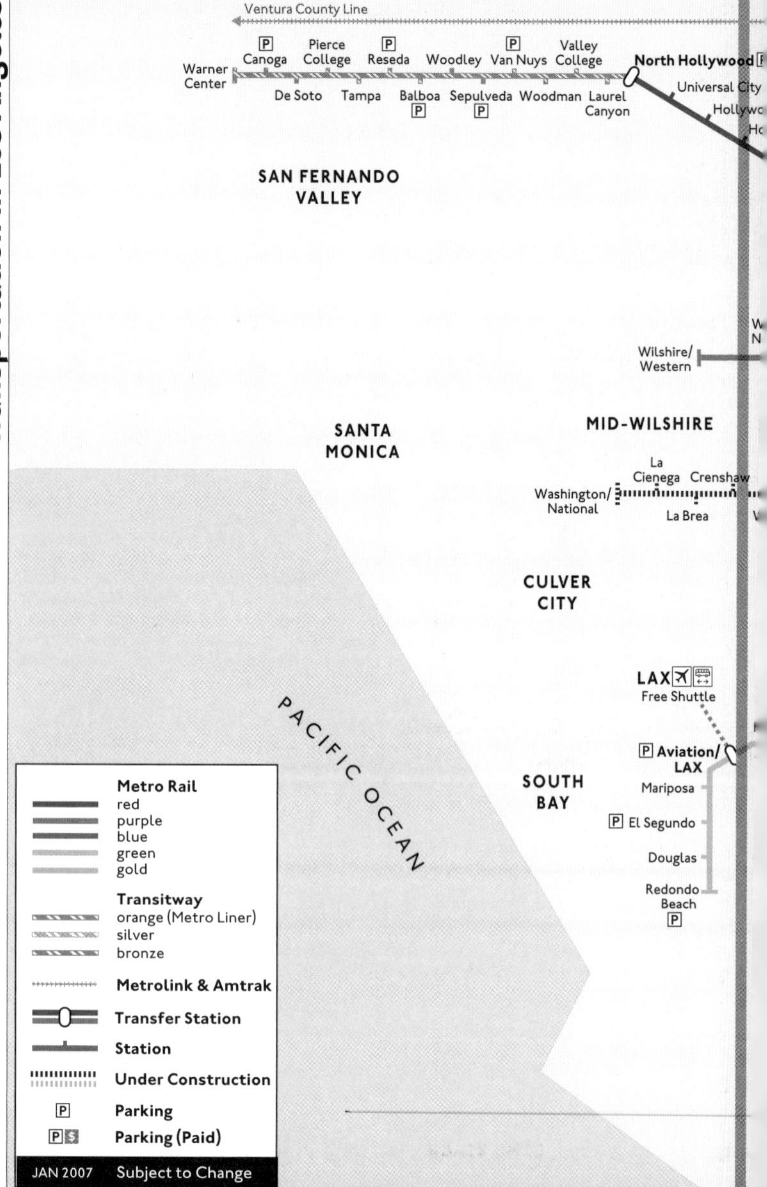

Ventura County Line
Warner Center
Canoga
De Soto
Pierce College
Tampa
Reseda
Balboa
Woodley
Sepulveda
Van Nuys
Woodman
Valley College
Laurel Canyon
North Hollywood
Universal City
SAN FERNANDO VALLEY
Wilshire/ Western
SANTA MONICA
MID-WILSHIRE
La Cienega
Crenshaw
Washington/ National
La Brea
CULVER CITY
LAX
Free Shuttle
PACIFIC OCEAN
Aviation/ LAX
SOUTH BAY
Mariposa
El Segundo
Douglas
Redondo Beach
Metro Rail
red
purple
blue
green
gold
Transitway
orange (Metro Liner)
silver
bronze
Metrolink & Amtrak
Transfer Station
Station
Under Construction
Parking
Parking (Paid)
JAN 2007
Subject to Change

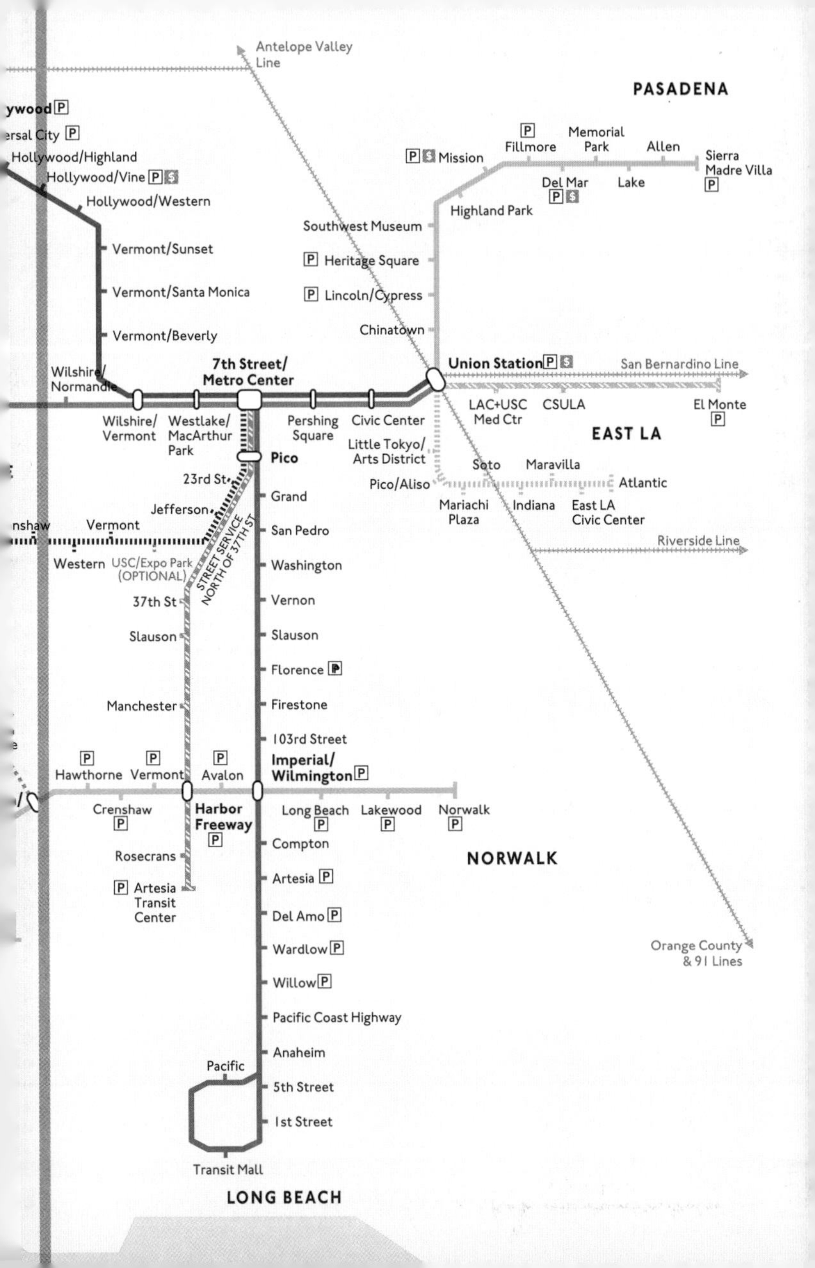

Antelope Valley Line
PASADENA
ywood P
ersal City P
Hollywood/Highland
Hollywood/Vine P S
Hollywood/Western
Vermont/Sunset
Vermont/Santa Monica
Vermont/Beverly
Wilshire/ Normandie
7th Street/ Metro Center
Wilshire/ Vermont
Westlake/ MacArthur Park
Pershing Square
Civic Center
Little Tokyo/ Arts District
Pico
23rd St
Jefferson
nshaw
Vermont
Western
USC/Expo Park (OPTIONAL)
STREET SERVICE NORTH OF 37TH ST
37th St
Slauson
Manchester
Grand
San Pedro
Washington
Vernon
Slauson
Florence P
Firestone
103rd Street
Imperial/ Wilmington P
Hawthorne P
Vermont P
Avalon P
Crenshaw P
Harbor Freeway P
Long Beach P
Lakewood P
Norwalk P
Rosecrans
P Artesia Transit Center
Compton
Artesia P
Del Amo P
Wardlow P
Willow P
Pacific Coast Highway
Anaheim
Pacific
5th Street
1st Street
Transit Mall
LONG BEACH
NORWALK
P S Mission
P Fillmore
Memorial Park
Allen
Sierra Madre Villa P
Del Mar P S
Lake
Highland Park
Southwest Museum
P Heritage Square
P Lincoln/Cypress
Chinatown
Union Station P S
San Bernardino Line
LAC+USC Med Ctr
CSULA
El Monte P
EAST LA
Soto
Maravilla
Pico/Aliso
Atlantic
Mariachi Plaza
Indiana
East LA Civic Center
Riverside Line
Orange County & 91 Lines

IVING

ar is the most
cient way to navigate
city, and the roads
often battered and
gested. Peak hours
7–10am, 11.30am–
pm and 4–7pm.
dworks are also a
quitous impediment.
*v. sigalert.com, http://
icinfo.lacity.org*, KFWB
AM or KNX 1070AM
o will give you up-to-
-minute freeway
ditions.
eed limits
*55mph on freeways;
45mph on surface
ets; 25mph in residen-
neighborhoods*
king
difficult to park and
areas provide free
king in municipal
. Availability and cost
a lot and it is
ential to read posted
is that indicate when
king is restricted.
ers range from $1–
r. Privately owned
ages can charge a
entrance fee. Most
aurants offer valet
vice around a
sonable $5. Central
els may charge $25–
a day for parking.
is
y tend to congregate
side airports, bars
clubs. In general,
easier to call a taxi
vice for pickup. Only
authorized taxis
a 'permitted
icle' city seal.
cker Cab
el. (800) 300-5007
ow Cab
el. (800) 808-1000
ependent Taxi
el. (800) 521-8294

METRO LINER

ON THE ROAD IN BEVERLY HILLS

and Skybar, an open-air lounge with matchless views of L.A., all epitomize the Sunset Strip scene. $295–395.

Four Seasons Los Angeles (**E** C1)
→ *300 S Doheny Dr (3rd) Tel. (310) 273-2222*

Beverly Wilshire (**E** B1)
→ *9500 Wilshire Blvd (Rodeo); Tel. (310) 275-5200 www.fourseasons.com*

Of course, Beverly Hills would have two options for the Four Seasons loyalist. The Doheny site is nestled on a quiet residential block; the Beverly Wilshire, a 1928 legend, recently underwent a $35 million face-lift. Both locations offer impeccable service and style. From $385.

Shutters on the Beach (**G** B4)
→ *1 Pico Blvd (Ocean Front Walk) Tel. (310) 458-0030; www.shuttersonthebeach.com*

Right by the beach, this Cape Cod-inspired hotel feels intimate and familiar, like a summer rental in the Hamptons. The concierge can set you up with a beach cruiser or schedule surf lessons. There's also free yoga on the beach, a fitness center – or just head straight for the luxury spa. From $335.

SLS Hotel at Beverly Hills (**E** D1)
→ *465 N La Cienega Blvd (Clifton); Tel. (310) 247-0400 www.slshotels.com*

Entertainment group SBE's first foray in hotels opened in 2008. Philippe Starck's whimsy fills the space, so yes, those are Plexiglas deer busts in the lobby and teacup-shaped chairs in one of the 297 rooms. Expect a scene – at the rooftop pool by day, and everywhere else at night. From $394.

PUBLIC TRANSPORTATION

Most of L.A.'s transport system is run by the L.A. County Metropolitan Transportation Authority (MAT, or 'Metro,' *www.metro.net*) and includes:

Metro Rail
Five light rail lines: blue, gold, green, red, purple. Extensions to Beverly Hills, Santa Monica and west of La Brea Avenue are planned for 2010.

Transitways
Three rapid bus lines: silver, bronze and the newest, orange, also called Metro Liner.

Timetables
→ *4am–1.30am (2am blue line); every 10–20 mins*

Metro Bus
Over 200 bus lines run east-west, north-south;
Metro Local (orange): covers the whole city.
Metro Rapid (red): fewer stops, faster journeys.
Metro Express (blue): serves high-traffic destinations during rush hour only.

Timetables
→ *5/6am–8/9pm (12.30/1am for Metro Local); every 10–20 mins depending on day of week; every 40–60 mins for Metro Express*

Fares & rates
→ *$1.25 single; $1.75–2.25 for Metro Express (exact fare required on buses); $5 for a day pass sold by bus driver or vending machines*

Other networks
Among the more used is the Metrolink rail commuter system, which serves Greater L.A.
→ *$4.75–12.50 single; enables you to connect for free on the Metro system*

RAIL STATION

Union Station (**A** D4)
→ *800 N Alameda St*
Meeting point of Metro Rail and Metrolink lines (see Public Transportation, right) and Amtrak long-distance train lines (*www.amtrak.com*).

BUS STATION

Greyhound Main Terminal (**A** D6)
→ *1716 E 7th St (Wilson)*
Tel. (213) 629-8401; Station open 24/7; Mon-Fri 8am–10pm (customer services); www.greyhound.com
Daily bus departures to Mexico and North American cities.

L.A.'S FREEWAY NETWORK

METRO STATION

TAXI

alcoholic) minibar is complimentary. From $196.
Hotel Erwin (**G** C6)
→ *1697 Pacific Ave (Windward)*
Tel. (310) 452-1111
www.hotelerwin.com
Casual and funky, the hotel feels more like a beach house; a new café restaurant and rooftop lounge – Hash and High, respectively – underscore the irreverent lifestyle of nearby Venice Beach. From $189.
Hyatt Regency Century Plaza (**E** A2)
→ *2025 Avenue of the Stars (Constellation)*
Tel. (310) 228-1234
http://century plaza.hyatt.com
The curvilinear edifice was built as the keystone of Century City. A favorite of Nixon and Reagan, once called the 'White House of the West Coast' has most recently been championed by the National Trust for Historic Preservation. $199–239.

$200–300

Ambrose Hotel (**G** A2)
→ *1255 20th St (Wilshire)*
Tel. (310) 315-1555
www.ambrosehotel.com
The award-winning and LEED-certified eco-boutique hotel is not only socially conscious, but also a real beauty. Dark woodwork and Mission-style furniture complement the Craftsman design. No valets or bellhops but patrons can be shuttled around in a biodiesel-fueled London taxi. $209–219.
The Langham, Huntington Hotel & Spa (**H** D4)
→ *1401 S Oak Knoll Ave (Wentworth); Tel. (626) 568-3900; http://pasadena. langhamhotels.com*
This resort, a 1906 Spanish-Mediterranean gem, was extensively renovated in 2008 and boasts 380 rooms, luxury suites and cottages, Michelin-star dining, an extensive full-service spa, and 23 acres of beautifully lush grounds. From $219.
Avalon Hotel Beverly Hills (**E** C2)
→ *9400 W Olympic Blvd (Canon); Tel. (310) 277-5221*
www.avalonbeverlyhills.com
The seductive hourglass-shaped pool now seems an homage to former resident Marilyn Monroe. Famed stylista Kelly Wearstler first staked her claim in hotel interiors here, creating a cool midcentury vibe with installations of Eames, Noguchi and Nelson. $260–290.
Sunset Tower (**D** C3)
→ *8730 W Sunset Blvd (Sherbourne)*
Tel. (310) 659-8290
www.sunsettowerhotel.com
Paul Fortune oversaw the interior redo of this 1929 Art Deco building on the Strip. Stylish modern rooms in beige, taupe and brown with spectacular views; great bathrooms. Restaurant is hugely popular; the pool is cozy for breakfast and lunch; spa and gym. From $275.

$300 AND ABOVE

Mondrian (**D** D3)
→ *8440 Sunset Blvd (La Cienega)*
Tel. (323) 650-8999
www.mondrianhotel.com
Philippe Starck put this über-stylish hotel on the map and Benjamin Noriega-Ortiz has recently redesigned it in keeping with Starck's surrealist mantra. Asia de Cuba with indoor/outdoor dining, the sleek deck and pool

Street names, monuments and places to visit mentioned in this guide are listed here alphabetically. They are followed by a map reference of which the initial letter in bold (**A, B, C**...) relates to the district and matching map.

Streets